THE CALL OF
KILIMANJARO

THE CALL OF
KILIMANJARO

FINDING HOPE ABOVE THE CLOUDS

JEFF BELANGER

imagine!

An Imagine Book
Published by Charlesbridge
9 Galen Street
Watertown, MA 02472
(617) 926-0329
www.imaginebooks.net

Jacket design by Cindy Butler
Interior design by Jeff Miller

Library of Congress Cataloging-in-Publication Data
Names: Belanger, Jeff, author.
Title: The call of Kilimanjaro : finding hope above the clouds / Jeff Belanger.
Description: Watertown, MA : Charlesbridge Publishing, 2021. | Summary:
    "A story of physical, mental, and spiritual transformation; an honest look
    at one man's mid-life; and a journey to the peak of Mount Kilimanjaro,
    the world's largest free-standing mountain"—Provided by publisher.
Identifiers: LCCN 2020021424 (print) | LCCN 2020021425 (ebook) |
    ISBN 9781623545116 (Hardcover) | ISBN 9781632892386 (eBook)
Subjects: LCSH: Belanger, Jeff—Travel—Tanzania—Kilimanjaro, Mount. |
    Mountaineering—Tanzania—Kilimanjaro, Mount. | Kilimanjaro, Mount
    (Tanzania)—Description and travel.
Classification: LCC GV199.44.T342 B45 2021 (print) | LCC GV199.44.T342
    (ebook) | DDC 796.52209678/26--dc23
LC record available at https://lccn.loc.gov/2020021424
LC ebook record available at https://lccn.loc.gov/2020021425

Printed in China
(hc) 10 9 8 7 6 5 4 3 2 1

All interior photographs are printed courtesy of the author, except for the photo on page 52, which is courtesy of Susan Belanger; the photos on pages 54, 87, 101, 104, and 129, which are courtesy of Brian Wyka; and the photos on pages 106, 159, 184, and 187, which are courtesy of Christine Whitmore.

IN LOVING MEMORY OF CHRIS

CONTENTS

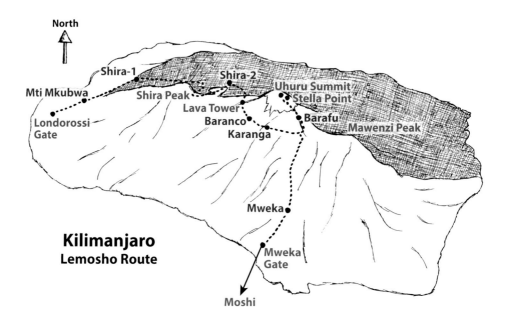

North

Shira-1

Mti Mkubwa

Londorossi
Gate

Shira Peak

Shira-2

Uhuru Summit
Stella Point

Lava Tower

Baranco

Karanga

Barafu

Mawenzi Peak

Mweka

Mweka
Gate

Kilimanjaro
Lemosho Route

Moshi

PROLOGUE

IT'S JUST AFTER THREE in the morning, and I'm as cold as I've ever been in my life. I'd estimate we're at around the 18,000-foot level. I can't breathe. I'm fighting for every molecule of oxygen. I suck in air as deeply as possible, but my face is so cold. I cover my mouth with a mask for warmth, but then I can't get enough air. I alternate between warmth and breath.

I'm back in my childhood, suffering through an asthma attack—my ribs ache from the strain of deep inhaling. It's dark. The only light is a hazy, tan halo around my feet from my headlamp. My body is sore from six days of climbing this mountain, and from my muscles screaming for more oxygen. I don't think I can go any higher. It would kill me to get this close and turn back. Yet pressing on could also kill me. We've already passed two plaques marking where people have died.

I can't help but question (yet again) why I'm doing this. Between gasps for air, I think about my brother-in-law, Chris.

When cancer took him just over a year ago, he was only a few years older than I am now. I'm doing this in his memory, but if I'm being completely honest, I'm mostly doing this for me. I'm testing myself at a time in my life when I'm otherwise in a rut.

Every step is part of that test. I lift my right foot higher on the mountain, then my left, pushing through air that's growing thinner by the step. But that's the only way I know to reach the top: one step, then another.

Time bends and stretches on this mountain like clay worked in the potter's hands. Was it only six days ago since I took that first step, somewhere far below?

KILIMANJARO NATIONAL PARK
TANZANIA

2,100 meters above
sea level (6,890 feet)
FROM LEMOSHO GATE TO:
Mti Mkubwa: 7 km
Shira 1 Camp: 14 km
Shira 2 Camp: 24 km
Moir Hut: 34 km
Baranco Camp: 34 km
Karanga Camp: 39 km
Barafu Camp: 43 km
Uhuru Peak: 48 km

1 MONDAY

LEMOSHO GATE TO MTI MKUBWA

I HAD IMAGINED what the first step of this journey would feel like. I had thought about taking a photo or video of that monumental footprint so I could show everyone back home how I would put my foot down with authority at the beginning of the six-day climb to Uhuru Peak—the highest point on Mount Kilimanjaro. But in truth, I am fifty yards up the trail before I can wrap my head around the fact that we're on our way. My T-shirt is already wet with sweat beneath my backpack. My water bottle bounces from my right hip as it swings from the carabiner attached to my pack. Beneath the midafternoon equatorial sun, the temperature around seventy-five degrees, the African forest makes its way into my retinas, slowly coming into focus as if I've emerged from a dark cave into bright sunlight.

It's fitting. My mind is as scattered right now as it was back home. I think about the work I'm missing. I feel selfish for taking this time and money away from my family. I ask myself if

The view of Mount Kilimanjaro from the roof of my hotel in Moshi, Tanzania—
my first in-person glimpse of the mountain.

I'm physically and mentally prepared. Did I train enough? Did I pack everything I was supposed to? And why am I doing this, anyway?

I'm a forty-two-year-old dad and husband. That's who I am. What I am. And it succinctly describes my life. My body isn't in perfect shape—I have the "Dad Bod"—because I don't get enough time for myself, I work a lot, and I struggle every day to find the balance between family, career, friends, health, and my own well-being.

Back at home in Massachusetts—more than 7,000 miles from here on Kili—my life has been a treadmill. Wake up, work, family, sleep, repeat—a rut. It's a rut of my own design, but a rut none-theless. There have been plenty of days when I only get about an hour of quiet after my daughter goes to bed. And considering how much spinning around my typical day entails between deadlines and appointments, an hour isn't enough time to delve inside and try to shine some light on that wide-eyed inner kid I once knew, who had questions about everything and wondered about big stuff.

Jack Kerouac wrote in his 1958 novel *The Dharma Bums*, "In the end, you won't remember the time you spent working in an office or mowing your lawn. *Climb that goddamn mountain.*" I get it. Shoot, I got it when I first read it years ago, before marriage and family. That doesn't mean I've always heeded the advice.

But you can stare at a mountain for only so long. Eventually, you have to climb it. Usually a mountain is a metaphor for something big in your life. For me, at least this time, it's literal. Mount Kilimanjaro is *my* mountain. Kili has called me for years, but this time I'm answering. At 19,341 feet, it's the tallest peak on the African continent. Sitting just south of the equator in eastern Africa, on the border of Tanzania and Kenya, it's the largest free-standing volcano in the world.

This is the region where, almost three million years ago, the earliest ancestors of the human species first walked out of the Great Rift Valley to begin their endless journey to wander the Earth. Their task: be fruitful and multiply. And multiply they did! Now there's billions of us. No wonder I feel lost in a sea of people at times. I can't help but rub my belly button and consider its former connection to my mother, and her belly button's former connection to her mother, and so on, and so on, all the way back to somewhere near here in Tanzania.

That kind of time frame creates perspective and makes me wonder why I'm making this trip. Cosmic enlightenment? Finding my inner child again? Maybe it's to prove something to myself and to others. Or maybe it's because the Maasai people in the Serengeti refer to the summit as the "House of God," and I'd really like to meet the creator of all of this.

I stumble on a rock in the path, which pulls me back to the moment of walking up this meandering dirt trail, engulfed by a lush, dense, green forest in a strange land. I laugh. It's a good stumble. I've been staring in wonder and not paying attention to the ground. Plus, the trail is well groomed and not overly challenging just yet. My misstep is nothing to be embarrassed about. I stumbled because the forest and reality of Kilimanjaro are sinking in.

My high school English teacher, Mr. Clark, didn't mind swearing in front of students. He was old, white-haired, balding, and loved Guns N' Roses—in short, he was one of my favorite teachers. He said there are two kinds of people: the first are those who look down all the time and see shit everywhere. By looking down, they avoid stepping in it. The second consists of people who look up: they see the scenery, but they're bound to step in some shit along the way. At home, I often look down to avoid the shit. Here on Kili, I just had my first step in shit—I stumbled on a rock and I'm grateful to fall into the category of people who take in the scenery, even if just for this moment. Still, the summit calls to me. The goal. The objective. How fast can I get there?

Christine, who is hiking behind me, asks if I'm okay.

"I am," I say.

Most stories don't begin with a profound moment. They just start. You jump into a movie already playing and trust you'll be able to catch up with the plot. So I'm asking you to jump in here, fifty yards in. When I forget to notice my first stride on Kilimanjaro. Not only have I not stopped to smell that rose, I didn't even see the damn thing. It's taken a stumble to remind myself of the gravity of what I'm doing.

In reality, my first step wasn't fifty yards ago; it wasn't back in Moshi, Tanzania, this morning; it wasn't back in Boston three days ago, when I boarded the plane for this trip. It was years ago—so far back that the memory is hazy, and in this moment on the mountain, it's no longer relevant. I'm here because of a million steps I took before right now.

In 1936, Ernest Hemingway published the short story "The Snows of Kilimanjaro." I didn't get around to reading it until two weeks before I left, as I was packing for Africa. There's a line in the story that stopped me in my tracks. When pondering the trip to the Serengeti, Hemingway's narrator says that he has come to Kilimanjaro hoping "in some way he could work the fat off his soul the way a fighter went into the mountains to work and train in order to burn it out of his body."

Work the fat off his soul.

I pray that somewhere on this mountain in front of me, I will lose the fat—the emotional baggage I've carried from childhood, the petty, personal issues and insecurities that I still lug around. I want to leave them here along with my footprints. Yet I don't plan to leave *everything* on these trails. I want to rid myself of the bulk, like wringing the water out of a wet towel but leaving the condensation that defines me. I'm the sum total of my scars and my triumphs. I don't want to change those things.

THE AIR FEELS A LITTLE thinner now. Maybe it's my imagination, or maybe my subconscious is calculating my elevation and comparing it to places I've been before—like Estes Park, Colorado, at 7,522 feet above sea level. Standing still in Estes Park, I didn't feel a difference. But when I walked briskly up a slight incline, I was as winded as if I were jogging. Right here feels a little like that; I walk through a rolling sea of deep-green ground cover and huge, towering trees that stand like ancient sentinels along the road to enlightenment.

There's something about a dense forest. I feel like I'm walking through the internal organs of nature. As if the woods are lungs and the trees are bronchi filtering the air. I'm walking through the middle of this great organism, and I can't tell if I'm in a symbiotic relationship or if I'm viewed as an inconvenient parasite or bacterium that somehow got into the system through grand design or dumb luck. The trees and shrubs stare at me curiously, as if they're trying to figure out if I'm a threat or a harmless passerby.

The very act of walking is primal. I'm doing what humans do. What we've done for hundreds of thousands of years. We keep moving because there's so much to see. Because we know from nature's example that all living things must keep moving. If a shark doesn't swim, it dies. And I'm not that far removed from our ocean-dwelling cousins. As I walk, I'm buffeted by a range of emotions: wonder, fear, awe, guilt, pride. Although training for this adventure over the last eight months has burned some fat off my body, it's the fat on my soul that's my concern now.

I hike past trees and foliage much like the forests back home in Massachusetts, but I notice subtle differences. New England woods have evergreen, maple, oak, white birch, and other hardwood trees. Here on Kilimanjaro, the trees have similar size and leaf cover, but a second glance reveals the differences—more mys-

Lush, green plants of the rainforest beneath towering East African camphorwood and yellowwood trees.

tery. The shapes and sizes of the foliage are different. Large vines hang from some of the taller trees, and the ground cover alternates between the familiar fern and other greenery that looks as foreign to me as I do to it. The woodsy, musk smell of the forest is familiar, but the sounds are slightly different. Birds, bugs, and other animals are chittering, but they're in the distance, chittering in their own African language—but not so drastically different from home that I notice them as anything other than background noise.

I keep walking. And thinking. Although I can't pinpoint the first step of my Kilimanjaro journey, I can mark a significant milestone on the road that brought me here: July 30, 2016, around seven in the evening. I was hosting an event at the Murdock-Whitney House in Winchendon, Massachusetts. I'm a paranormal guy. I write about the supernatural, ghosts, and legends for television, in books, and in public lectures, and I sometimes host events where I go to a historical place to raise money for the preservation of the location and allow the public to come in, shut the lights off, and hunt for ghosts.

If you're thinking, "That's the strangest way to make a living that I've ever heard of," you'll get no argument from me. It's not the kind of career one plans. I wanted to be a writer, but this subject drew me in because I love history, spirituality, psychology, and philosophy, and all of those fields of study intersect in what many call the paranormal. Exploring these mysteries has been a study of my own spirituality. But studying spirituality from the armchair can take you only so far. At some point, you need to dive into the muck to figure it out for yourself.

My self-employed life is filled with "have-to's." If I don't work, I don't get paid. I have a family counting on me, which is why I say yes to almost every project that comes my way. While that has kept beer in my fridge and pizza on my table, it leaves very little time for myself. I'm lucky that my work is also my passion because I get to explore strange locations and mysteries. But still, when someone pays you to do something, it's work.

So far, I've lived my life between the seen and unseen—the intangible, but still very real. Although I make a living in legends and the paranormal, in all other senses, I'm pretty . . . normal. I can change the oil in my lawnmower with one hand while waving "howdy, neighbor" with a beer in the other. I've swapped all the hardware on the toilets in my house at least twice since I bought the place, and I can look in the mirror and optimistically see a work in progress. I'm happy, but there's room for improvement. And of course, at times I get restless. There's got to be more to life, right?

At this event in Winchendon, we were wrapping up the dinner portion of our program when Amy, one of our regulars who works for the Leukemia & Lymphoma Society (LLS), said to me, "Hey, we have a new fundraiser you might be interested in."

I sighed. A few years ago, my wife, daughter, and I participated in one of the society's "Light the Night" walks in Worcester, Massachusetts, which involved walking on a city sidewalk for two miles while holding a balloon with a glow stick inside. Through social media, I was able to raise a chunk of change for LLS. It's a good cause, but the biggest physical accomplishment in that endeavor was that no one in my family had to stop to pee during those two miles.

When Amy mentioned they had a new fundraiser, my brain raced through excuses: *I'm so busy right now. I have multiple projects I'm trying to get through, more events, and my busy fall season is approaching. Of course, I want to help if I can, but there's only so much . . .*

"Mount Kilimanjaro," she said. She sat there smirking like she thought this was the coolest news ever. Her spiky, blonde hair and smiling face waited for my response. I was carrying two paper plates with some pizza crust on them, a soda can with a tiny bit of liquid still sloshing around the bottom, and some napkins. I had one foot on the threshold of the front door, as I was about to go inside to find the trash can.

Time slowed. I stopped midstride.

"Kilimanjaro?" I asked. But really, it was more of a statement.

The next day, I talked to my wife, Megan, about the short discussion I'd had with Amy the night before.

"I'd be gone for thirteen days. I'd have to train a lot between now and March, and it will cost us a lot of money for me to go," I said. (I don't believe in sugarcoating these things.)

Megan gulped. "I need a little time to process this," she said. "Let's talk about it in another day or two."

I've been married to Megan long enough to know that she's both supportive and open-minded, but it's not a good idea to try and back her into a corner for any kind of quick decision on big things. So I let it go. Meanwhile I pored over the information Amy sent me. The trip would cost about $4,500 (I'd learn later that the amount was optimistically low), and the climb would require six days up the mountain and two days back down. I would fly to Tanzania, stay in the city of Moshi for two nights, do the climb, spend two nights back in Moshi, and then fly home.

Two days later, Megan said to me, "I know you're going to do this. You have to. Just give me another day or so." I could tell by her smile that the green light was coming. She was genuinely excited for me. So I made the commitment to Kilimanjaro and fundraising for LLS a week after Amy told me about the trip. It was the day of my forty-second birthday.

THE FIRST LEG OF OUR ASCENT is the seven-kilometer hike to Mti Mkubwa Camp. As I climb, memories of my preparation for this adventure flash through my head like abrupt cuts in a grainy movie: running extra miles on my treadmill, watching my diet, training with the group from LLS with our coach, spending hundreds of dollars on gear, telling everyone I know I'm going to climb Mount Kilimanjaro—and knowing that telling them will further compel me to go through with it. My concerns—that I was exercising enough, hiking enough, that I was focused enough—are all becoming irrelevant now. I'm just a guy walking up a hill. One step, then another. Left foot. Right foot.

Today's hike to the first camp is only four hours. It isn't a test of my limits or endurance. Not yet. As the movie reel fades from my mind, Africa comes back into clear focus: greenery around a well-maintained dirt trail that winds upward, around hills, to higher places I have yet to see. Something deep inside me starts to tingle. I look around and feel like I'm finally part of this new forest, no longer looking at it the way you see a zoo animal through cage bars; I'm *in* it as I follow the trail and follow our guides. The trail dips down by a stream, then back up a steep hill. Then another Africa moment: sounds of a foreign, yet not unfamiliar language, Swahili.

WHEN AMY TOLD ME about the fundraiser eight months earlier, she couldn't have known it, but Kilimanjaro had been on my bucket list for years. In my college years, at Hofstra University, I had a foreign language requirement. At first I took French because I had studied it throughout high school, and my family heritage is French. But my French is *merde*, as they say in Paris, and I failed my freshman class. Having to change course, I switched to Spanish, but the two languages are so close that I was confused. I passed, but barely. *Dios mío.*

When I lamented to a friend that I needed to take a language unlike French or Spanish to fulfill the language requirement, she said, "You should take Swahili. I took it and loved it. Plus, the professor is awesome."

"Swahili?" I asked. "Where do they even *speak* that?"

"Mainly Tanzania and Kenya in eastern Africa," she told me.

It sounded weird. And historically speaking, weird and I have gotten along, so I signed up for the class my sophomore year.

"When the hell are you ever going to use Swahili?" my mother asked me over the phone.

"You never know when I'll be in a mall someday and someone will yell out, 'Does anyone here speak Swahili?'" I told her. (Full disclosure: this has yet to happen to me.)

And my friend was right: the professor was awesome. You know how throughout your years of school and college, there are those rare amazing teachers who make a big impact on you? My Swahili teacher was one of them. Dr. Robert Leonard's background was as interesting as the language and culture he taught. Going into his class, I already knew about Dr. Leonard's former career, but it was more fun to hear him talk about it himself—a story that he would tell within the first week of every semester of his teaching career. He told the story—as he had so many times before and still does, I'm sure—with well-polished aplomb, but the heart behind it made it ring as true as the first time he related the tale.

It was the first day of class. In his melodic baritone, he greeted us in Swahili. "*Hujambo*," he said, a term I would soon learn was a formal greeting. As Dr. Leonard was describing what we could expect from his course, a hand in the classroom sheepishly rose. Anticipating the question, Dr. Leonard smiled.

"Yes?" he said.

"Dr. Leonard," the student asked. "Is it true you used to be the lead singer of Sha Na Na?"

Sha Na Na was a doo-wop group that started up in the 1960s and eventually went on to have their own television show. Dr. Leonard smiled, put down his syllabus, leaned back against his desk, and said, "Okay, let's do this now."

He explained how he was the cofounder of the group, how he performed at Woodstock—going on right before Jimi Hendrix—wearing a gold lamé suit, and how he toured all over the world with them. But in 1977, even though the group had landed a television series, he'd had enough. He left the group and moved to Kenya to find himself and to teach English. He wound up also learning Swahili and falling in love with the people and culture there.

I was hooked. I not only took Swahili I, but Swahili II. We learned about the many greetings, the terms for the young, the old, and the middle-aged, and also about the culture of those who spoke the language and a little bit about the great mountain, Kilimanjaro. But no, of course I'd never actually have the need to use the language for myself . . . *would I?*

THE AFTERNOON SUN filters through the trees and canopy above. Twelve of us, plus seven guides, are making our way up the Lemosho Route toward Mti Mkubwa. The point where we had started a few hours earlier was 6,890 feet above sea level, hundreds of feet higher than the tallest mountain I've ever hiked back home. At 6,288 feet, New Hampshire's Mount Washington is the tallest peak in New England. But here on Kilimanjaro, we're just getting started. Two hours into the hike, I figure we've gained close to another thousand feet in elevation.

The twelve of us were strangers to each other a year ago. It was the LLS that brought us together for this trip. Five of us are from New England. Each of us signed up through LLS and agreed to raise funds to fight blood cancer. The first person I met from the group was Christine. Back in November, as we were loading up our gear and starting our first training hike into the Blue Hills of Boston, I said to her, "So let's get the elephant in the room out of the way first—we're going to be pooping together on Mount Kilimanjaro."

She didn't miss a beat. "That's right," she said. "Behind trees, rocks, or just out in the open. There will be no pride left."

I knew we'd get along. In the coming months, we talked a lot on those training hikes, led by our New England coach, a man we affectionately called "Sherpa Tom." Christine was a personal trainer and an orphan. She lost her mother to lymphoma, and her father died shortly afterward, mostly from a broken heart. This cause haunted her, which made this experience deeply personal.

Then there was Gayle, who I met on a training hike to Mount Monadnock, in southern New Hampshire. She was in her mid-fifties, and a year earlier, she had been bald from chemotherapy treatment for acute myeloid leukemia. She received a lifesaving bone marrow transplant in September 2015, and there we were hiking Monadnock together only fourteen months later. So I pretty much thought she was a badass out of the gate. Maria was from Connecticut. She was in her forties, short, bubbly, new to hiking, and taking on a big challenge. She joked that her name was pronounced "Ma-rear" because she often brought up the rear.

Finally, there was Brian, who was my roommate at the hotel in Moshi and would be my tentmate on the mountain. He was tall

The approach to the summit of Mount Monadnock in Jaffrey, New Hampshire.

and wiry, with dark hair flopped back on his head. He was a young guy, twenty-eight years old, and it was obvious at first glance that he was in the best physical shape of all of us. (He had to cut one of our training hikes short so he could go on a twenty-mile bike ride—yeah, *that* guy.) I cracked a few jokes with him about being stuck in a tent with me and my body smells at high altitude, and he laughed. He was pretty easygoing; I knew we'd be fine.

The other seven in our group were mostly new to the New England gang. Jason joined us from New Jersey. Although I was meeting him for the first time in Tanzania, he had been on a training hike with Christine and Maria on Mount Greylock, in the Berkshires of Massachusetts. Belinda, Vanessa, Shannon, Suzanne, Nancy, and their coach, Robert, hailed from California. I was also meeting them for the first time on this trip.

OUR PACE IS UNNATURALLY SLOW. If we were walking in front of you on a crowded city sidewalk, you'd be yanking at your hair and groaning in frustration until we got out of your way. Picture Grandma with a walker . . . OK, slightly faster than that, but still too slow for my usual taste. "*Pole pole,*" our guides say. Although the word looks like *pole*, it's pronounced "poe-lay" and means "slow" in Swahili.

"This is way too slow," one of the California contingent complains.

I look at Christine, "It's not like we have something else to do today, right?"

She laughs.

"What time does the Starbucks close at the camp?" I ask.

Another snicker.

I'd also like to be moving faster, but I trust our guides. Others in our group make comments about our speed. I take it as good news that we're all in good enough shape to move up these hills. A few hours in, this is starting to feel like a normal hike, not the early stage of an epic journey. The forest, which just a couple of hours ago seemed foreign, has already become familiar. I recognize the trees now the way you start to recognize landmarks in a new neighborhood. Then, around four o'clock, some movement in the trees reminds me, we ain't in Massachusetts anymore, Toto.

Our guide suddenly stops to point at the branches above. I don't hear what he says at first, but our line of twelve pauses, and we look up to our left. Twenty-five feet or so in the air, the branches of one of the towering, leafy trees are moving.

"Monkeys!" Christine says. She points ahead, her mouth locked in a big smile.

I dig my camera out from the top of my backpack and aim in the general direction of the movement. If I were hosting an animal documentary, I'd likely get fired right now. *There's wildlife . . . over there . . . or maybe there.*

I click blindly, hoping my new camera will capture more than my naked eye. I'm told there are blue monkeys up there. A branch wiggles, some leaves sway and draw my attention, and I see a small, monkeylike shape. I zoom in tight as the monkey takes only a mild interest in our group.

Our guide, Mark, turns and points at another tree ahead of us. More monkeys, but these are bigger. There's two of them, black with bright white tails. They look like large skunks from a distance, but Mark tells us they're white-tailed colobus monkeys.

IT'S MY FIRST SIGHT OF A MONKEY in the wild. Monkeys, of course, are our ancient ancestors. We once competed for the same resources on equal footing. Seeing them in zoos does not compare. They lack freedom, and they depend on humans for their food and their very survival. Out here, they are free to go where they want. The thought that one could leap on my face in some kind of primate rage passes through me, but only for a second. Thirty feet above us, they're not bothered by our presence. The colobus monkeys move around the large tree like it's a jungle gym on the playground, swinging from one branch to another, and I click pictures. Of monkeys. In Africa. *This is cool.*

With each new step, the countryside feels more like another land. There are no wild monkeys in New England. I'm grinning like an idiot, walking through the forest of Kilimanjaro and

A blue monkey stares unconcerned at our group as we tread into his realm.

clicking pictures like some cheesy tourist. Where's a fanny pack when I need one?

I hit Christine's arm. "Dude! We're on Mount Kilimanjaro!"

The trail so far is well defined, groomed, and neatly marked with logs at the edge. It's considerably easy, especially compared to many New England trails I've hiked. No big rocks to navigate—just a walk in the park, really. If my friends back home could see me now, they would *not* be impressed with the physical challenge I'm facing today. But I'm not doing this to impress them. Okay, I'm not *only* doing this to impress them. But I do think there are some bragging rights in this for me.

Our head guide, Augustine, stops the hike to introduce us to a new term. "We going to stop and pick a flower," he says. His English is soft-spoken, slow, clear, and deliberate, but his Tanzanian accent flavors every word. Augustine is on the short side, always smiling, with a gentle way about his speaking and the manner in which he carries himself.

"Pick a flower?" I ask.

"If you need to make pee, you can find a spot around here," he says.

"Pick a flower." Mountain-speak for "bathroom break." Being only a few hours into the first day, it's only a pee break. But I know what's lurking in the shadows ahead—we all do. You may not think about it when you are back home, but once you're up on that mountain, in those wide-open spaces, your most private moments become *very* public. The theme from *Jaws* cues up in my head.

The trail climbs, dips, and makes its way lazily up the far western slope of Kilimanjaro through the forest. The trees are tall, so there's no view below, and no summit anywhere to be seen either. We're gaining several thousand feet in elevation, though I don't feel it in my breathing. As we climb one last slope, orange-domed tents are revealed in the clearing in front of us. We've arrived at Mti Mkubwa Camp. *Mti Mkubwa* means "Big Tree" in Swahili. It's aptly named, as there are many large trees in and around this camp. As our group enters the clearing, our porters and guides assemble in front of us. They sing in Swahili, clapping and dancing. The songs transport my wandering mind back to right here, right now.

When the music hits me, I'm not worried about home, not worried about being perceived as a rich white American, not worried about climbing the mountain. *Hakuna matata.* No worries. These voices, the songs, the music hits my soul. It's *joy.* That giddy feeling that starts in my upper chest and radiates out.

Christmas morning as a child, opening presents. All of us join in, singing and clapping.

"*Zina, Zina,*" our guide Sunday calls out.

"*Zina,*" the rest of the porters and guides sing in unison. "*Zina*" refers to a woman's name. It's a tribute song to the girl you desire. You can always swap out Zina's name with the name of the object of your own affection. Sunday is stocky, with a strong, clear voice that he's honed in church choirs throughout his life. His left hand has clearly been through some kind of accident, because his fingers are scarred and bent in an unnatural way, but the old injury clearly doesn't bother him or slow him down at all.

Sunday calls out a line, and the men respond in song. There's no one among the guides and porters who doesn't know the words. They've been singing these songs their whole lives. The men are dressed in well-worn clothes, which I can tell have been donated because many don't fit quite right. They serve their purpose of coverage and warmth—nothing more. Some of the men jump in place to the rhythm of the song; others sway back and forth. All of them act like humble ambassadors to their language, their mountain, their songs, and their culture.

The songs continue for close to ten minutes. Then the crew members introduce themselves. Between the two head guides, Augustine and Wilfred, the assistant guides, cooks, waiters, camp crew, and porters, there are forty-eight altogether. All of them are from Tanzania. And there are only twelve of us. The guides speak perfect English in addition to their native Swahili and are the highest-paid people on the expedition. Next come the assistant guides, then the two waiters, and finally the porters who do all of the heavy lifting and transport our tents and camps from site to site for us.

My personal porter's name is Wilfork. He carries my 140-liter dry bag each day and helps set up my tent before I get to camp. Wilfork speaks no English, but he has a big, bright smile.

I'm expected to carry my backpack, which weighs about fifteen pounds, plus my day's water, accounting for another four pounds or so at the start of the day. My sleeping bag, clothes, cold-weather gear, and toiletries are in the dry bag that Wilfork carries, which I borrowed from my friend Melanie back home. She used the same bag a few years ago to summit this mountain—so I figure it's got some luck in it.

My personal porter, Wilfork. Though he speaks no English, we find reasons to smile and laugh.

As the porters finish introducing themselves, a black-and-white colobus monkey appears a hundred feet or so behind us. Someone from the California group points and remarks how cute he is, but the porters, who know better, are already sprinting toward him. The furry bastard grabs a loaf of bread wrapped in plastic and darts back into the forest, easily escaping with the loaf for his trouble. Another good lesson—everyone and everything in Tanzania seem to feed off this mountain in some way. I can't blame the bandit for grabbing a free meal. The monkeys appear to have no interest in getting close to people. I'm more afraid of insects—specifically mosquitoes—thanks to the warning given to me by my travel doctor two months ago.

My travel doctor is Dr. Hanumara Chowdri, an old Indian man whom I had met only once thanks to a referral from my insurance company, when I went to him for shots and prescriptions to prepare for my trip to Tanzania. After my tetanus, hepatitis B, and typhoid shots, he prescribed Diamox to make life easier at high altitudes, and something for diarrhea because if that hits while I'm on the mountain, dehydration could become a life-or-death issue. Finally, he prescribed Malarone for malaria. Although I'll mainly be in the mountains, above the tree line, it takes only one bite at lower elevations to make me too sick to climb or do anything else. The doctor told me to start the Malarone a few days before I leave for Tanzania, and take it for at least a week after I return. The same for the Diamox.

Then he removed his glasses and took a breath, which gave him a solemn air. "I have to tell you this," he said, a little uncomfortable. He paused. "Don't have sex with anyone over there. HIV is very prevalent in Tanzania."

I smiled. Sex was *not* in my plans. But it was a reminder that if I happened to find myself around someone profusely bleeding or something like that, I would need to be aware. Then the doctor had something else to say, in the same somber tone.

"How tall is Kilimanjaro?" he asked

I told him, "19,341 feet," and then smiled, because I'd been rattling that number off for months.

"Have you ever been that high?"

"I've been to 9,000 feet in Colorado," I said.

"This is very different," he said. "If you can't breathe, if you're too sick, you'll need to come back down."

I nodded politely. He left the room. I didn't fear this trip until that moment. Rolling an ankle, a big fall and a broken leg—these are things I'm aware can happen on any mountain. But one little bug bite that could place me in a hospital, or if my body couldn't handle the altitude, they were now on my list of fears. More doubts crept in too.

Here at camp, I know it's still warm enough for mosquitoes, though I don't see or hear any. Brian and I are assigned to Tent 3. My dry bag is already inside. The tent is bright orange, oblong, and about three-and-a-half feet high. I suppose it could sleep three people if you had no gear. Most of us will be two-to-a-tent. Brian has camped a lot. I, on the other hand, would rather cut off a finger than camp in a tent.

I'll get dirty with you all day long. I'll hike from sunup to nightfall, I'll sweat and rough it all you want, but damn if I don't want a hot shower and clean bed by the end of that day. No such luck here. Brian sets up his sleeping bag and sleeping pad first, while I wander around the camp and take pictures.

Our first camp at Mti Mkubwa, which means "Big Tree" in Swahili.

I'm looking for something to do, in a familiar and compulsive way. I walk around the camp and take pictures of anything that grabs my attention. One of my biggest faults is that I'm overly goal-oriented. I'm all about the destination, not the journey. I'm not proud of that, but it's a fact. It's also something I'm working on. I bought this fancy new camera as a way to remind myself to capture moments along the way. So I wander through camp clicking pictures. I'm trying to see simple things from different angles.

Although there's plenty of room for other groups at Mti Mkubwa, there's no one else in our camp besides our team.

"How come we're the only group here?" I ask Augustine.

"This is the last week of the season," he said. "The rainy season starts, so no Kili for few months."

The rain. It's something I've prepared for, but also something I dread. I have the gear, but water has a way of seeping into every nook and crack. It makes the ground slick and dangerous. But when I glance up, the cloudless sky allays my rain fears for the moment. There are a few large trees in the middle of the clearing, the ground is mostly level and dirt, and there are a few buildings, including a rusted metal relic from about fifty years ago and a small brick structure that looks like it can't be more than ten years old. Inside the building are holes in the ground for dumping human waste. Large trees encircle the camp like sentinels and grow darker as the light fades.

Back in Tent 3, it's my turn to set up. I have a self-inflating mattress pad that I also borrowed from my friend Melanie. While it's blowing up, or rather slowly unrolling itself and getting slightly thicker as air fills the inside, I unroll my bright yellow, zero-degree sleeping bag, which is like a ski parka with a hood, and then blow up my inflatable pillow with my mouth. I squeeze the mattress pad after closing the valve. Is this going to keep all 195 pounds of me off the ground? I'm skeptical of this whole setup.

Months ago, the national coach for the LLS Climb 2 Cure program suggested via email that we sleep outside in our sleeping bags for a night or two at home to get used to them. Purposely, I did not. I would have hated trying to get comfortable in my sleeping bag in my backyard, knowing that my warm, clean bed was less than twenty yards away. That would make my first experience in my sleeping bag a bad one. I figured I'd wait until I was on the mountain, until my bag was my very best option for the night, so I'd learn to love it. That was my plan. And I don't regret it. But right now I'm wrestling with this stuff. The mattress doesn't feel like much of a mattress. It's a far cry from my pillow-top, super-duper, wonder coil, mega-awesome bed at home.

When we aren't wearing them, Brian and I keep our stinky boots in the vestibule area of our tent.

As a matter of policy, Brian and I agree to leave our boots outside the tent in its tiny vestibule area, covered by a small triangular tarp. As I pull my boots off, my nose immediately tells me our plan is a good one: our boots already smell. I switch into some sneaker-type shoes I brought and finish repacking my bag, setting it between the sleeping bags next to Brian's so that they form a barrier. With a wall of gear between us, there's no danger of someone getting inadvertently spooned.

Back outside, the Mti Mkubwa Camp sign lays out the journey ahead.

MTI MKUBWA CAMP

Elevation: 2,650 meters
above sea level (about 8,700 feet)
Vegetation Zone: Montane Forest

FROM MTI MKUBWA TO:
Shira 1 Camp: 7 km
Shira 2 Camp: 17 km
Baranco Camp: 27 km
Karanga Camp: 33 km
Barafu Camp: 37 km
Uhuru Peak: 43 km

A porter sets a bowl of warm water and a crumbly bar of soap by our tent. I scrub my hands and splash my face in the water. I'm used to hotel sinks, so for me, this is roughing it. Still, I don't feel dirty yet. This cleanse hardly feels necessary, but I figure it's better to take advantage of luxuries when they're offered.

The view is obscured by tall trees all around me, but the clearing offers an opening above it that shows the sky turning from pink to deeper blue as the sun sets somewhere far away.

A large, yellow-domed mess tent has been erected for us. It looks space age—like something you'd see on a Martian landscape. Inside, a series of folding metal tables and chairs have been set out for us to eat dinner. Our porters have carried all of this up here for us. It seems extravagant given the circumstances, but as

Our mess tent with more creature comforts than I expected—a welcome sight after an afternoon hiking to Mti Mkubwa Camp.

I settle into a chair with the rest of the climbers, I'm grateful for the creature comforts.

I also see real plates and silverware. Not wedding china, but still, metal silverware and thin, ceramic plates. There are salt and pepper shakers, other condiments, napkins, and anything else you might pack for a cabin or a vacation home. In my mind's eye, I see a number above each item on the table. A weight. It doesn't matter if that number is ounces, pounds, or kilograms—it's mass that must be carried by someone. No wonder we have a small army moving with us up this mountain.

Our waiters, Victor and Philbert, bring out a soup course first. It's a salty but delicious vegetable soup that's mostly broth. Next, they bring us rice, fish, and some green beans. My food expectations coming here were low. Considering that we need to carry all the food we eat with us, I envisioned eating trail mix for days on end. The soup and actual dinner are a treat. Given where we are and what we're doing, my only concern with calories is not getting enough of them. Anything consumed will be burned in the hike.

"*Tam sana*," I say in Swahili, "Yummy, delicious."

During this first dinner on the mountain, our group of twelve discuss some of our fundraising efforts. Each of us had to raise a minimum of a thousand dollars for the LLS, or else cover the grand ourselves. Most of us raised much more than that.

"I was shocked both by who donated and who didn't," I say. "There were people I didn't know that well who ponied up hundreds of dollars. Others I know very well, and who I also know have the means, gave nothing."

Gayle says she has a wealthy friend who told her, "If I gave to everyone who asked, I'd be broke."

Not a great attitude. Two years ago, I made a New Year's resolution to give money every time someone asked me. At the grocery checkout, "Would you like to donate to Children's Hospital?" "Yes." A homeless person on the street, Girl Scouts selling cookies, a solicitor at my door for charity. I said yes every time and gave something, yet I'm not broke. I'm not a rich person, and I couldn't afford to give hundreds to everyone who asked, but I can give something every time. Living that way for a year made me feel good. I gave every time. So I continue to do it.

I'm not perfect, but I like how giving makes me feel. Sometimes I miss something, or I have no cash on me, but otherwise my rule is to give because I was asked. I figure the universe put that person in front of me for a reason, and I'm here to help when I can and how I can. During my fundraising efforts so far, I've had donations from over three hundred people, with an average donation of around fifty bucks. Some people gave five. I'm grateful to all of them. Giving anything was a gesture I deeply appreciate. Before I left for Tanzania, I printed the list of donor names on a piece of paper that I carry with me in my pack. It doesn't weigh much, and I figure it's the least I can do for them.

People parted with their hard-earned money because I asked them to. I don't take that lightly. It really is the thought that counts. It shows some effort of support. Not once did I look at any person's donation and think, "Is that all? Come on, you can do better." Gayle's story reminded me how easy it is to clam up and focus only on yourself. I have disdain for that attitude because it's easy for me to see it in myself. That karma stuff? It's real. All the good stuff comes back, and it comes back a lot quicker than you think. I try to focus on the good stuff because of how it makes me feel.

President Abraham Lincoln once said, "When I do good I feel good; when I do bad I feel bad, and that is my religion." I get it.

After we finish dinner, I step out of the mess tent into the twilight. I can see the tents, but there's only minutes of daylight left before night falls completely over our camp. The first few stars twinkle to life. There's no campfire or anything like that; the plan is to get to bed soon because tomorrow is going to be a long day. "We going to get up at six-thirty, eat breakfast at seven-thirty, and move out by eight-thirty," Augustine tells us in his slow, deliberate way, chewing each word as he translates it in his head to English.

Although there's little light left in the world, the forest is alive with funky, foreign noises. Monkeys call to each other, bugs and other animals join in the cacophony, and yet the sounds seem in the distance, as though these creatures know to give our camp a wide berth. Vanessa and Belinda, from San Francisco, are in the tent next to us. They have brought battery-powered Christmas lights to put on their tent at night. I laugh at the notion of carrying the extra weight for something so frivolous. But as Mti Mkubwa grows dark, the lights look pretty damn cool. Why miss an opportunity to add flair?

Vanessa and Belinda drape their solar-powered lights over our tents. What I initially thought was frivolous turns into Kili-fabulous.

As I'm brushing my teeth near the edge of the woods, I look up through the tree branches and admire the clarity of the stars. They shine brighter than I've ever seen before. I can only imagine this view when we get above the tree line. As I awkwardly climb into the tent, hunched over, trying not to fall face first, I see that Brian is already in his bag, ready for sleep. I try to zip the door of the tent closed and end up splitting the zipper so it's open in gaping spots. I struggle with the zipper, and Brian sits up to assist. I'm helpless at camping—I can't even navigate a zipper! Brian laughs, I laugh, but I still recognize I'm behind the curve on this. I wonder what else I may not be prepared for.

Undressing while lying down is something I'm not used to. I slide my hiking pants down and slip on my track pants and a T-shirt. I flip over to try and get into my sleeping bag opening, and my ass hits the packs between Brian and me, sending my backpack tumbling on top of him.

"Shit! Sorry, man," I say. I pick the pack up and put it back where it was. I half fall into my side of the tent as I try and get my sleeping bag open enough to crawl in. From the outside, I can only imagine how the shaking tent must look to the guides and porters. From the outside, it either looks like Brian and I are getting along *way* too well, or it looks like a battle between a tent and its occupant, and the occupant is losing.

Still, I manage to navigate inside my ski parka of a sleeping bag. I'd guess the temperature outside is in the fifties, so this bag is a bit too warm. I try to zip up, but only get the zipper halfway up before it sticks on something. I'm *not* going to bother Brian again for another zipper. Leaving the bag half open makes sense anyway because in these temperatures, it may get too hot inside.

I position my inflatable pillow under my head and try to get comfortable on the hard ground.

I know that inflatable mattress pad is under me, but damned if I can feel it right now. Brian has all of his gear and clothes organized into neat plastic bags. Everything is precisely in its place, and I feel like the guy who uses industrial garbage bags for luggage. If we're the camping odd couple, I'd be Oscar Madison.

Once Hurricane Jeff gets settled inside Tent 3, I listen for a few minutes to the sounds of the monkeys in the distance, and the sound of some of the guides and porters moving around camp. I don't feel exhausted, but I know the week I have ahead of me. Have I trained enough to handle this? Am I strong enough? Fit enough?

EIGHT MONTHS AGO, when I started training for Kilimanjaro, I wasn't starting from zero. I would place my zero back to the winter of 2007, when my daughter was eight months old. I weighed 245 pounds, the most I've ever weighed in my life. When you have a newborn, it's kind of . . . *uhhhm* . . . exhausting? Debilitating? All-encompassing? All of the above?

I slept very little. I felt like a zombie in a fog. I worked, I changed diapers, I tried to take care of the house and chores, and the very last person I took care of was myself. At my lowest point, I needed something for dinner in the early evening. My wife was upstairs taking a nap. However bad it was for me, it was worse for her because she was nursing. My daughter was also napping, and I had emails and phone calls to return. But still, I needed food. I ate not one but two packages of Twinkies for dinner as I sat at my desk typing. Although the sugar bombs made my inner child squeal with delight, my adult self felt gross. I ran my hands along rolls of belly that didn't used to be there. In that moment, I decided that I would start running.

I'm not now, nor have I ever been, built like a runner. I'm stocky and broad shouldered. I never enjoyed running. Why run if no one was chasing me? And if I was in such a hurry, no doubt a car would get me where I was going faster. We had this treadmill in our basement that Megan used. She *is* built like a runner and would peel off miles on that thing before our daughter was born. So I slipped on some shorts, a T-shirt, and my old sneakers, and down I went to the basement, iPod in hand.

I pushed the miles per hour up to 3.5, thinking I'd start with a brisk walk. Soon I pushed it up to 6 miles per hour and huffed and puffed. I made it just past a quarter of a mile before I had to slow it down to a walk again. My lungs were hurting. My calves and legs were also burning, and I was sweating. After walking for another couple of minutes, I pushed it up to 6 miles per hour again. I was angry and focused, but only in short bursts. I made it another quarter-mile and backed it down again to a fast walk.

When I hit a mile, after about thirteen minutes, I shut down the treadmill in an exhausted pant. I was ready to collapse. I sat on the floor in a heap next to that machine of torture and terror trying to catch my breath, sweat dripping off my brow. It would be easy to blame my asthma and go back upstairs and try dieting. But that day I didn't. I decided to run again.

I made running a regular part of my life. I didn't love it. Hell, I didn't even *like* it. But I did it because soon I could run that mile without stopping, and then two miles. I ran every Monday,

Wednesday, and Friday, and my weight dropped. I paid more attention to what made my body feel good. What made me sleep well at night. Just listening to my body, I ate better: less sugar; fewer carbs. And I kept running. I changed the way I was living. In about a year and a half, I dropped fifty pounds and felt better about myself. One very strange by-product of all of this running was that my asthma became almost nonexistent.

After that, I ran for health maintenance. I even took part in a few 5K races. Then work would get busy, and I'd cut down on my exercise time. But once I committed to Kilimanjaro, I never slacked off. No matter how busy my day was, I ran, I lifted weights. If I got tired and wanted to quit early, I would ask myself if that would help me get to the top. Plus, LLS gave us some exercise recommendations to help us train. Planks daily, training hikes, push-ups, and other activities to prepare my body for this endeavor. I did all of it.

The summit of Kilimanjaro gave me a fitness goal like I'd never had before. I didn't want to fail. It's estimated that about 35,000 people attempt the Kilimanjaro climb each year, and only 60 percent make it to the summit. According to one guide company, approximately one thousand of those people need to be evacuated from the mountain, and about ten people die. I don't want to fail. I definitely don't want to die. So I trained, I hiked almost every weekend, and I dreamed.

I REACH INTO MY BACKPACK for my iPod, knowing that music will help me relax and clear my head. I scroll through my old eighties playlist and cue up "Africa," by Toto. I loved that song as a kid. As the drumbeats begin the tune, there's that giddy tingle in my chest again. Africa. Kilimanjaro. *I'm here.*

A few lines from the song call out to me for various reasons. The writer in me loves this one: "I stopped an old man along the way / Hoping to find some long-forgotten words or ancient melodies / He turned to me as if to say, 'Hurry boy, it's waiting there for you.'"

That's what writers do. We look for songs yet to be sung. Stories that haven't been told. I'm here in part for that reason. For me, finding a good story feeds my soul. Even though I've chased thousands of stories throughout my career, they're mostly other people's stories. I'm the teller of *their* tales. But this story is my own.

The other line hits closer to the rock-hard mountain under my back right now: "I know that I must do what's right / As sure as Kilimanjaro rises like Olympus above the Serengeti."

"I bless the rains down in Aaaaafrica . . ."

I take a deep breath and try to sleep.

2 TUESDAY

MTI MKUBWA TO SHIRA 1 CAMP

MY EYES OPEN to a dull gray color in the tent. Light is beginning to leak into the world. I'm sure I slept some, but not a lot. My lower back is sore. This bag and sleeping pad were *not* enough to keep a 195-pound man off the ground. No position felt right last night. I tossed and turned. I've experienced sleepless nights in hotel rooms before, so for the long periods when I was awake, I concentrated on my breathing, on clearing my mind and resting my body.

It's very late . . . or early . . . I can't tell, but I think I'm the only one awake in camp. Doubts creep in again: Am I cut out for this? Do I belong in a hotel where I can look at the mountain through a telescope? Have I gotten soft in my middle age? Can I do six more nights of this? Will I make it to the top? Is that the real goal?

I once had the opportunity to interview Mark Inglis for a children's book I wrote a few years ago called *What It's Like*. Inglis is a mountaineer who holds the record for being the only person to summit Mount Everest *without legs*. He lost his legs below the knees to frostbite many years ago. He didn't quit living, and he didn't quit mountaineering. He told me, "When you reach the summit, you have to remember you're only halfway there. You still need to get down."

Mark is right, of course. I can't think of the summit as the singular goal. If I don't come home to my family, that is true failure. I lie here in tired frustration, trying to imagine my goal not being the summit. I can't right now. The concept is too foreign to my entire makeup as a person.

No one has to wake us up. When you go to bed at eight-thirty, you can only stay down so long, especially when sleeping on the ground. And it's getting lighter outside. Brian is also awake. I put on a baseball hat and crawl outside our tent. Everything has that early-morning gray hue to it. Like the colors haven't quite come out yet because they're waiting for the sun. The air is sharp, like an early fall morning.

I turn around and see that our tent has been draped in toilet paper. I know immediately it was Vanessa and Belinda. I thought there was something about them I liked. TP'ing our tent on the first night. Well done.

Although I didn't sleep well, I'm renewed at daybreak. The rising sun offers another chance at all of this. I know from experience that I can always skip a night of sleep and be okay. But I also know that I can't skip two.

After getting dressed, Brian and I take turns packing our bags with our sleeping bags and clothes. I let Brian pack first. It's an easier process when you have some elbow room. He packs as efficiently as he unpacked last night. Brian told me that his no-shower

Well done, Vanessa! TP'ing our tent on the first night.

record is two weeks, when he hiked a section of the Appalachian Trail. So he knows about minimalist packing and stinky living.

I, on the other hand, camped in high school when sleeping over at Ed Zang's house. We set up tents in the woods, some girls we knew did the same, and people snuck alcohol from our parents' liquor cabinets. There was a campfire, underage drinking, and desperate teenage attempts to hook up (the attempts failed). By morning, we all went back to the comfort of our houses.

This is worlds different. I'm trying to roll my sleeping bag. You'd think it was some mighty python fighting for its life. She would lift her head and I would bear-hug her back down to the ground. I'd get her rolled up halfway before she springs to life again and comes undone. Everything is a struggle, but somehow, some way, I get my stuff packed into the 140-liter dry bag, which now feels like a giant rubber garbage bag.

With my bag placed on the tarp the porters have laid out, I walk into the mess tent for breakfast. For breakfast, they serve us porridge, fried eggs, toast, and fruit. It's clear I won't go hungry on this trip. I eat everything because I love breakfast, and I'm grateful when someone else makes it for me.

Wilfred checks my vitals. He clamps a red device onto my finger and we wait for the results. My oxygen level is 87 percent, my heart rate is 56. He asks me the same series of questions he asks the rest of the group: How do you feel, on a scale from 1 to 10? I say 9 because I didn't sleep that well. Did you pee in the last two hours? Did you shit in the last twenty-four? Yes to both. Although one of those occurred in the hotel the previous morning—I have yet to christen the mountain.

Are you taking Malarone? Diamox? Yes to both. Malarone to stave off malaria should I come in contact with an infected mosquito, Diamox for the altitude. Any coughing? Shortness of breath? Dizziness? No to everything. These levels are checked twice daily to make sure that no one is suffering from altitude sickness or any other signs of illness that could quickly escalate into an emergency. It's another reminder that climbing a mountain is a serious endeavor. There's no elevator back down if I get sick or hurt.

After my health check, I feel a rumble in my bowels and know it's time. Dear God, it's time right now!

There is an outhouse-sized tent that's been put up for us at camp, and inside is a squatty potty, which campers may be familiar with. It's a toilet, about eighteen inches tall, that dumps into a little compartment below. It's surrounded by an outhouse tent that zips shut, but it's pretty clear what's happening in there.

I know we're getting ready to set off for the day, and I'd rather deal with this here than in nature's toilet. Pride be damned, and with no magazine or iPhone to pleasantly distract me, I do my business into the compartment. . . . In a juvenile way, I just conquered another mountain. No sense getting too worried about personal privacy! I grab my backpack and join the others at the trailhead.

We're moving again. Although I'm a little sleepy, I feel invigorated by the new day. There's a chill in the air, but one that I can tell will disappear quickly as the sun climbs. The air is still, and there are a few clouds lazily crawling above us. But not that far above us. Back home, I live around two hundred feet above sea level. Clouds in the sky are way out of reach from that perspective. Here, it feels like I could almost reach them with a stepladder.

The landscape looks much the same as it did yesterday. We're still following a well-marked dirt trail through the forest, with no view up or down because the trees are so tall and dense—though there's more pale-green lichen growing on these trees, which mutes the dark green of their foliage more and more as we ascend. Soon there will be hardly any color at all as we move above the treeline.

Our head guide, Wilfred, leads us, pointing out more monkeys in nearby trees. Within the first hour, our porters pass us, carrying green tarp bags on their heads and shoulders. The bags are watertight and contain our entire camp. They're moving ahead of us to set up the next camp.

"*Jambo, jambo!*" we say cheerfully as they pass.

"*Jambo,*" they say back. Sometimes a high five, sometimes a fist bump.

As we ascend on our first full day of hiking, the colors drain from the foliage. Muted green lichen hangs all around us.

"*Mambo, poa,*" another says. Which means something like, "Hey, cool," in Swahili slang.

I was fortunate to grow up near the woods. My friends and I would walk through the forest, build forts there, and spend countless hours exploring. As a kid, I figured I could walk forever. It never seemed to tire me out. Today is no different. Christine and I tend to walk together. Over the months of training, we've become friends (I call her my "trail wife"), and we also both talk a lot. In the occasional silences, I nudge her arm and say, "Dude, we're *still* on Kilimanjaro!" In reminding her, I'm also reminding myself.

My mind drifts to the summit. It's something I want badly. It's why I'm here. But it's also days away. I work to suppress my goal-oriented nature. As the time and steps plod on, and Christine and I retreat into our thoughts, I think back to another reason I'm making this journey. Cancer. It's the cause we're raising money for; it's a factor in my life.

CANCER. It's a motherfucker to be sure. I lost my paternal grandfather to cancer. My other grandfather also had it, though it didn't kill him. My father has had skin cancer, and fifteen months ago, I lost my forty-six-year-old brother-in-law, Chris, to cancer. That wound is still fresh in my family.

Two years before his death, Chris was having some ongoing stomach issues and unexpected weight loss, so he went to see his doctor. He was only forty-four; no one was expecting anything major. The doctor ran some tests, and then some more tests. The results looked strange, so an MRI was arranged. In October 2013, his doctor called him at work and told him to come over to his office right away. As in, don't make an appointment, don't wait until your workday ends—come now.

Chris knew that doctors don't typically roll that way, so he headed over to the office assuming there wasn't good news waiting for him. What he didn't know was just how bad the news would be. Tumors. Lots of them. And all over. Initially it was colon cancer, but it had already metastasized to his lungs and liver. "Eighteen to twenty-four months," the doctor told him.

The funny thing about two years is that it's both a long time and not a long time. It's like driving through the desert toward a far-off mountain. You keep driving for hours, but the mountain doesn't seem to be getting closer . . . until finally it does. Because the desert offers you little perspective, the mountain looks big from a distance, but it looms over you suddenly when you finally do approach it.

Chris and I weren't close when he first married my sister, but we always got along. He was funny, and he became a regular fixture at family gatherings. He was familiar. But he was like me in a way—tough to get close to. It took me until middle age to realize that about myself. I don't let a lot of people in. Chris was similar. Not rude or standoffish, just hiding behind a wall of laughter. I got that.

But cancer, and its death sentence, changed everything. Suddenly I could no longer count on getting closer to him at some point in the future. There wasn't much future left. So our family rallied around Chris. We checked in with him a lot, and our kinship grew. Because of my work writing about the supernatural and paranormal, Chris knew he could talk about things with me that he couldn't talk about with my sister.

It was both a special and a horrible time. Chris's life changed in an instant with the news; over the next year and a half, he would lose his job and most of his quality of life. He was in pain and suffering from depression. A friend of mine who works in hospice care said to me, "People die the same way they live," meaning that if you grab life by the neck, that's how you'll treat the dying process. If you're more one to sit back, that is how you'll die. Chris would have said that he was fighting his illness, but in reality he gave up almost from the moment of the diagnosis. He wasn't much of a fighter in life, and he wasn't doing so in death. I was disappointed in him and the example he was setting for my nephew. It's not a disappointment I could share, because I can't say how I would act given his death sentence.

I'd like to think I'd go down swinging. I hope to God I never have to find out.

In August 2015, for my birthday, I received two tickets to a preseason football game between the New England Patriots and the New York Giants. The Giants were Chris's favorite team. And since I was born in Massachusetts, the Patriots were mine. I called Chris and asked if he wanted to go. He was touched and thrilled. At this point, his health had deteriorated pretty badly. He could still walk short distances, but he needed a wheelchair to get around. So I would have to wheel him to the stadium, return the

With my brother-in-law Chris at a football game. Though we rooted for different teams, we both enjoyed the four-hour break from Chris's nonstop cancer life.

wheelchair to the car, then run back to the stadium (and do all this in reverse when it was time to leave). Chris was a little embarrassed at having to be pushed in a wheelchair, but in every other way this was a great day for him, and for me too. He wore his Giants shirt into enemy territory, and of course, I wore my Patriots gear.

That evening, we talked football. We talked life. We didn't talk about cancer or the inevitable mountain that was looming somewhere on the horizon. But Chris knew that this would be the last time he saw his Giants in person—even if it was mostly the scrubs playing in the preseason. And the Giants' scrubs beat the Patriots' scrubs 17–9, so Chris was happy. I hid behind the "it's only preseason and it doesn't matter anyway" shield.

September faded into October, and Chris grew thinner and weaker. By early December, he was hospitalized for complications stemming from his organs slowly shutting down. He already had multiple tubes surgically implanted in his abdomen to drain the fluids that his liver and kidneys could no longer process, but even those tubes weren't keeping up anymore.

So there we were. It was December 2015—two months past Chris's predicted expiration date. I received a text from Chris the day after he went into the hospital: "Do you have time to talk this morning? I don't know anyone else I can talk to about this."

That morning, we talked on the phone for a while about some out-of-body experiences that Chris had been going through almost every night since the previous week. The first one scared him—only because he was so high up, he felt he would fall. He said that he felt like he was twenty feet in the air, which doesn't make any sense because the ceiling of the room couldn't have been more than ten feet high (plus, he confided, he'd always had a fear of heights). But the second experience, *that* was incredible. He couldn't control his movement, but he was aware of being out of his body. He said that it felt both electric and free.

This would turn out to be the week that Chris made peace with what was happening to him. Six days after our phone call, the doctors sent him home for hospice care. "There's nothing more we can do," they said. "Liver failure is imminent." The mountain now loomed high and heavy above us. I went to see him at his home on Saturday, December 12. For two days, he had been lying in a rented hospital bed in his bedroom. His skin and eyes were yellow from jaundice, but in the afternoon sunlight that flooded through his bedroom windows, he looked golden. I know this color is unnatural for a human, but somehow it worked for Chris. He was enlightened. Radiant even. But still dying.

His oxygen machine offered a low hum—a steady rhythm in the room, broken up by his occasional awkward breaths. His lips and mouth were dry, making speech difficult. But still we talked. For three hours, we talked.

I asked him about the out-of-body experiences, and he said, "Oh yeah, they're still happening. But now it's several times a day. And now I'm seeing . . . *things*."

"What do you mean by *things*?" I asked.

"The first time I was out of my body, standing in my bedroom, and I saw my cat from childhood." He paused. "The funny thing is, I haven't thought about that cat in probably thirty years. I never even liked him!"

I laughed. Then he continued, "But I also saw my grand-mother."

"Did she say anything to you?"

"No, she was just there. I'm always very conscious to not try and force anything to happen during these episodes. I want to let the experience unfold on its own."

"What do you think these out-of-body experiences mean?" I asked.

"The best I can figure is that there's something inside this broken machine getting ready to wiggle out and stay out."

He wanted me to know. And he wanted me to tell others. This guy, who wasn't quite an atheist when I first met him, was going through a deeply spiritual experience. He was walking the cliff's edge toward the supernatural. Step by step.

For most of us, death happens in an instant. You're here. You're gone. A car accident, a heart attack, going to bed one night and not waking up—death surprises us in many ways. But Chris . . . Chris got intimate with death. For Chris, this had been a long courtship, a slow dance with the inevitable. He and death cohabitated. They got to know each other. In a way, it was a precious gift.

That Saturday, we talked about life, about death, and about this profound human experience he was going through. Chris was no longer numbers or test results, and he was definitely no longer a disease. He was a person again. A golden person, ready to embark on a new adventure.

As a stream of visitors poured through his doors, Chris had a gift for each of them. He was blessed; it was as if he were attending his own funeral, fully conscious. His friends and family got to say kind words to him. He graciously accepted them. There was no need for grudges anymore. No issues or grievances made any sense in those moments. There was no need for anything but kindness and love.

I sat there in awe of our conversation. I realized that I too was dying. Am dying. I have been since the day I was born. Although I'm in good health right now, I can't know if there's some runaway truck out there waiting for me on the highway of life. Or if one of my own routine doctor visits will turn into a death sentence. Or if somewhere ahead of me on a mountain somewhere, a misstep might mean my end.

My own mortality sunk in. Chris was only a few years older than me. That day, I received an abundance of gifts and blessings from Chris. Not just talking and connecting to a fellow human being, but being reminded by him that though I'm not counting my final hours, I'm still dying. Like him, there was no need for me to shut people out who may want to visit in whatever capacity. I learned this from a golden man whose spirit was already practicing leaving his body for his next journey. Two men sitting, talking, and dying together.

Chris passed away on December 20, 2015, in his home. My sister was by his side, as was my six-year-old nephew, Henri. Chris also left behind an older son, Colin, and a daughter, Courtney, from a previous marriage.

IN MY BACKPACK, I'm carrying a picture of Chris and a picture of Chris with Henri. In my head, I've promised to take them to the summit with me. I hope to keep that promise to myself. To Chris.

Chris and my nephew Henri, on their last family trip, a photo I carry with me on Kilimanjaro.

Behind me now, on the trail, a woman's voice pulls me out of the memory.

"This is too slow," she calls out to no one in particular. It's Nancy from California. The pace does feel slow, and if left to my own devices, I would likely walk comfortably at almost twice this speed, but I put my trust in our guides. They must be pacing us this slowly for a reason.

"*Pole, pole*," they say again in Swahili. Slow, slow.

Since we departed Mti Mkubwa Camp this morning, I can say with each step that this is the highest elevation I've ever hiked. Years ago, when I visited Cripple Creek, Colorado, the hotel I was staying at was 9,000 feet above sea level. Walking a short distance from the parking lot to the hotel, or up a hill, would leave me winded. But at the slow pace we're moving now, I don't feel winded at all. Not yet. I'm starting to understand. *Pole, pole.*

"I can't go this slow," Nancy whines again.

I make a move to put some distance between me and her. Her complaints are bringing me down. Also, I figure, "Where the hell else do you have to be today?" I try to put her out of my mind and focus on where I am and what I'm doing.

The landscape change is gradual as we make our way east up the mountain. It's sunny again, with temperatures in the seventies, and yet a crisp breeze is blowing around the mountain—a reminder of the altitude. It feels like an early autumn day back home. Warm, but that undertone of chill coming. The trees get shorter and more sparse, and at times I catch glimpses of the plains below the great mountain. The tree trunks are gray now, muted tones, and look half-tree, half-rock. These trees have no shame; they know that to live here, they're going to look weathered and haggard, and yet they're sturdy. It's as if they've learned to grow up harder than their cousins farther down the mountain. Maybe they look this way as a final warning to those venturing upward—this place can beat you down. Proceed at your own risk.

As we climb the next hill, we move into an open landscape where I'm taller than most of the grasses and shrubs. Rolling hills spread outward and upward for as far as I can see.

It's been almost two days since I've seen the prominent peak of Kibo, the highest point of Kilimanjaro, from our hotel in Moshi. As drab greenish-gray as the world around me is becoming, when I crest the next hill, the view far below Kilimanjaro more than compensates for the lack of aesthetic beauty in my immediate vicinity. To the north, I can now see far into Kenya. Fields of

As we gain elevation, the vegetation diminishes in size to reveal the rolling foothills of Kilimanjaro.

green and brown are like a patchwork quilt, and somewhere out there is the Serengeti, with its lions, elephants, giraffes, hippos, and so many other animals I've only seen in zoos. I'm on their turf now. Or rather, high above it. Where we are now, most animals and most people don't go.

Beyond the Serengeti, beyond Kenya, beyond the Indian Ocean is the rest of our planet. As I gaze at the view, I'm reminded of a quote by David McCullough: "Climb mountains not so the world can see you, but so you can see the world." There are birds and mice here, and various insects, but the climate is turning hostile toward life. The sparse trees are a warning to living things that we're entering another realm. Yesterday's hike was too easy—a literal walk in the park—but today I know I'm on a mountain.

I'm clicking pictures. A lot of them. I turn my head and want to remember everything. I want to burn the image into my permanent memory in the same way that my camera burns the image onto the memory chip. It's my effort to smell the roses. But my photos are also a trophy in a way, if I'm being perfectly honest. *Look where the hell I am!*

By lunchtime, we arrive at a hilltop where our porters have set up the mess tent again. White, iceberglike clouds drift by, paying us no attention. Some are so close that I feel a foglike kiss from them; others glide by in the distance. I'm among the clouds now. On their level. I ask Christine to film Wilfred and me puffing our cheeks and blowing toward the clouds so it looks like we're moving them. Wilfred and Christine oblige. I may be in Africa, but I'm still a dork.

Clouds drifting by on our way to Shira 1 Camp.

The rest of my life fades into the background of my mind. I'm not forgetting my family, job, or where I'm from, but right now I know this is where I'm supposed to be and what I'm supposed to be doing. I'm not defined by my occupation anymore, or the type of car I drive, or the address of my home. None of that matters. I trust that my family, which I hold dear, will be okay without me for a few weeks.

I wonder if this is how a dying man feels, how Chris felt at the end. God willing, near the end of life, I can only hope that if I see that abyss closing in, I will have the inner peace of knowing that I've done all I can, and that the people I love will be okay. I burn through a cycle of emotions here on this hilltop. I fight back a tear, and though I don't know where it comes from, I acknowledge that it's here for a reason, as I am. It's serving a purpose, even if I don't know what it is right now.

After a lunch of cooked, but very dried out—almost to the point of jerky—chicken legs, fruit, and candy, we press onward and upward. Still gaining elevation, still finding more magnificent views of the hills and valleys below. Africa opens up to me like a vast canvas as I gaze outward from the mountain. Seeing the summit of Kibo, the most prominent peak of Kilimanjaro, eludes me, and yet I trust it's there somewhere, waiting.

The landscape passes in muted tones of gray and green, with only a couple of exceptions. There are a few bright yellow and red flowers the size of my fist bursting open like little floral fireworks. Our guide Mark tells us this plant, called a *protea*, is the official flower of Africa. Although we see plenty of bushes that can bear the flower, seeing one in bloom is rare at this time of year—so the first one I see sticks out. I smell the flower, though I can detect no

The protea, the official flower of Africa.

fragrance. I touch the petals, and photograph them as close as my camera can get while remaining in focus.

The flower looks so fragile, and yet it must be hardy to live and thrive up here in the rocky soil and colder air. I love the contradiction this flower represents beyond its physical beauty. It reminds me not to take everything at face value.

I gaze up and see clouds moving around the deep blue sky. The inclines aren't so steep. We're winding our way along hillsides and ridges as the hours pass by on the way to Shira 1 Camp. I breathe. The air feels cleaner than it does at home—the way the air feels on an icy day, as if you can taste the oxygen without any particles in the way—except it's not frigid right now. Just clean. The azure blue looks pure and unspoiled. This may be the so-called Third World, but they definitely have a few things over us.

Farther ahead, there's another flower, a strange, bright red, orange, and yellow one that begs for a photographic close-up. I can pause only so long to click pictures because the train of people isn't stopping. We've been walking all day, and the sun is starting to make its way back toward the horizon.

As we follow the trail around the next hill ahead, a giant plateau opens in front of us. Far across it, and slightly to my left, huge, white clouds glide over and around a huge mountain. It's Kibo! The glacier-topped summit is up there, among the clouds.

Clouds parting on the Shira Plateau, offering my first view of the summit since leaving Moshi.

Kibo hides from us most of the time. The clouds part for only a moment, offering me a glimpse of the goal. Then more clouds move in, obscuring the summit. But dammit, it's *there*. My pulse quickens. I'm giddy. Here. Now. Kilimanjaro feels within reach, just a few miles across this plain. But it also appears far away—it's the dichotomy of mountain perspective. In the same way that two years is both a long time and not a long time. Also, this is a distance I'll have to walk. At my hotel in Moshi, I understood that I was technically on Kilimanjaro, but I didn't *feel* it until right now. The summit is within sight. Right there on the horizon, yet still days away.

As I'm clicking pictures, the animated clouds slide aside for me and then cover the coy summit once again. The clouds move so fast, it almost looks like a time-lapse video. Our guides want to keep moving. They point to a greenish roof on the horizon—Shira 1 Camp, our destination for today. But that mountain, she's called to me for years, and here I am. I can't help but stare and photograph her like some paparazzo.

I stumble on a few rocks because I'm not watching where I'm stepping. I'm strangely proud of that. I don't care. I'd rather look at the majesty of this place than worry about looking foolish on the ground. Another stumble, and I remind myself that while looking up to appreciate the beauty is wonderful, twisting an ankle won't help me right now. I know from experience that near the end of a day of hiking, your muscles and coordination aren't as good as they are at the beginning. It's easy to pop an ankle.

Shira 1 Camp sits on an expansive plateau. Most of the shrubs are roughly waist-high, boulders of the same size dot the landscape, and the clearing ahead is where our camp waits. As we approach, the clouds hiding the summit of Kilimanjaro drift aside again, like a curtain before a stage performance, and our guides and porters gather to sing to us, with the summit as their backdrop.

"Hujambo . . . Hujambo bwana, habari gani, nzuri sana
Wageni mwakaribishwa, Kilimanjaro hakuna matata."

The translation is:

"Hello, hello, sir. How are you? I'm just fine
Dear guests, be welcome to Kilimanjaro—not a problem."

Anyone who has ever seen the Disney movie *The Lion King* has heard a bunch of common Swahili words. *Simba* means "lion," *rafiki* means "friend," *nala* means "gift," and the most prominent song of the film, *"Hakuna Matata,"* does indeed mean "No worries" or "Not a problem." As I listen to the songs and the porters and guides speaking, I pick out more words I understand.

Some Asian dialects sound like songs, Slavic languages are more guttural, and Romance languages like French, Italian, Spanish, and Portuguese sound like poetry. But Swahili fits into all of these categories and none of them. There's a tempo and beat to the cadence that feel like an African drum; there's no dressed-up formality to the rhythm; it feels comfortable, like a friend. Neither is it intimidating. Although for that part, we must give credit to the people who speak it. They're warm and welcoming. They seem pleased and patient when we attempt to say a few words in their language. A line in the Kilimanjaro song goes: *"Hii ni lugha yetu jifunze pole pole, hakuna matata."* "This is our language, learn it slowly—not a problem."

When the singing stops, I look around to take in more details of my new surroundings. Bright yellow flowers are everywhere around us. The camp is spread out, but as with our first camp, there's no one here but our group. Unlike at Mti Mkubwa, there's a vast expanse in all directions and a big sky. The green roof that we had seen in the distance belongs to a shack where a single park employee sits with a ledger for each of us to sign in.

SHIRA 1 CAMP

Elevation: 3,610 meters
above sea level
(about 11,850 feet)
Vegetation Zone: Moorland

FROM SHIRA 1 CAMP TO:
Shira 2 Camp: 10 km
Baranco Camp: 20 km
Karanga Camp: 24 km
Barafu Camp: 28 km
Uhuru Peak: 33 km

I find Tent 3, and once again Brian and I take turns setting up our sides of the tent. Yesterday, I had thought I heard our guide Augustine say that there were extra mattress pads, so I ask him if I can have one. It turns out, that's not accurate. There are no extra, but that doesn't stop him from finding a porter who is willing to switch his big inflatable pad with my thin one. His mattress looks like one of those swimming pool floating cushions that you inflate with a hand pump. They're inexpensive, and suddenly I wish I had gone that route instead of borrowing Melanie's tiny, self-inflating mattress pad. Man, these guys are accommodating, but I tell Augustine there's no way I could switch with him. I wouldn't sleep a single minute the rest of the week from the guilt. I'll have to learn to live with my thin pad.

This time I don't rely on the self-inflating feature—I really blow into that mattress until it's as full as I can make it. I'm a little lightheaded from the process (and the altitude), but I'm determined to sleep tonight. I brought some sleeping pills just in case. I'm taking them tonight, no matter what.

Unlike yesterday, we still have a few hours of sunlight and some time before dinner. With Kilimanjaro sitting there across the plain staring at us, I can't resist grabbing my camera gear and setting up some shots. I also brought a GoPro video camera, and I set it up at the far edge of our camp so there is nothing between the lens and the mountain. I let it record. I want to document this every way that I can because that's what I do.

I'm stepping outside the moment now. I'm working. I struggle with that notion, but it's not much of a struggle. I want these shots. I want to capture the moment and beauty of what I'm seeing, even if only for myself. Once the camera is recording and I've snapped a few posterity shots, I have some time to look at the mountain with no one else around me.

I whisper, "You called, and I'm here . . . sorry it took me a while." I feel corny, but what I say is also true. It's like we're watching each other from across this plain. She is formidable. The mountain is sizing me up, asking if I'm worthy, if I'll make it. Being here staring at her, I understand why Kili is one of the famed Seven Summits.

THE SEVEN SUMMITS are the tallest summits on each of the seven continents. Climbing all of them gives you mountaineering bragging rights for life. The first to do them all was Richard Bass, who completed his quest with his Everest climb on April 30, 1985.

Here are the peaks Bass climbed:

- Antarctica—Mount Vinson (16,050 feet)
- Australia—Mount Kosciuszko (7,310 feet)
- Asia—Mount Everest (29,029 feet)
- Europe—Mount Elbrus (18,510 feet)
- North America—Denali (20,322 feet)
- South America—Aconcagua (22,838 feet)
- Africa—Mount Kilimanjaro (19,341 feet)

There's some argument over this list. Basically, it comes down to where you want to draw your borders. Mount Elbrus is in western Russia. If you don't want to consider that Europe, then it gets dropped from the list and you replace it with Mount Blanc (15,774 feet) in the Alps. And if you want to expand Australia to include the South Pacific, then you would add Puncak Jaya (16,024 feet) in Indonesia, and drop Mount Kosciuszko. But there is agreement on the rest of the summits.

As I said earlier, my previous climbing record was Mount Washington, at 6,288 feet. Native Americans called this mountain, located in the White Mountains of northern New Hampshire, Agiocochook, which translates to "Home of the Great Spirit." Anyone who has ever looked at this mountain and heard its call can understand why many people believe that there is a spiritual entity inside. It's the tallest peak in the northeastern United States.

The summit of Mount Washington is 4.1 miles uphill from the parking lot at Pinkham Notch, and it is one of the most challenging hikes I've ever done before Africa. The ascent is uphill all the way. There aren't a lot of switchbacks that allow you to walk level for a bit while staying parallel with the base, before turning uphill again to gain more elevation. With Mount Washington, you head up in varying degrees of incline. And the early parts of the trail are actually steeper than much of the later climb.

After two or three hours of navigating wobbly rocks and boulders, you rise above the tree line, through trails lined with small, hardy bushes, and then move on to nothing but a pile of giant rocks leading skyward. In places, you have to pull yourself up and over rocks the size of a car, as the wind whips by and the temperature plummets. The first time I hiked this mountain was shortly after college, during the summer. The temperatures were in the mid-seventies at the base and the lower forties at the summit. With only an extra sweatshirt in my backpack for gear, I was grossly underprepared for that hike.

To date, 150 people have lost their lives on Mount Washington. Many have died in the winter from avalanches, skiing accidents, or hypothermia. However, plenty of others have died in the summer. A memorial just below the summit marks where Lizzie Bourne of Kennebunk, Maine, died on September 14, 1855. Lizzie was hiking with her cousin, Lucy Bourne, and her uncle, George Bourne, without a guide. At that time, there was an inn called the Summit House at the top, so as daylight began to fade, they knew that if they could get to the top, they would have warmth and shelter for the night. But then . . . clouds and wind moved in out of nowhere, as can often happen in the White

Mountains. After all, Mount Washington is the mountain where the highest recorded wind speed on Earth was logged, on April 12, 1934. The wind clocked in at 231 miles per hour that day.

In a cold, cloudy fog, Lizzie and her other family members were separated. Confused, she stumbled along in her dress until well after dark, seeking any kind of beacon from the Summit House to lead her, but she never showed up at the inn. The next morning, her lifeless body was found just a few hundred yards from the Summit House. She died of exposure and hypothermia—in the summer. Hers is a lesson many others failed to learn: Don't trifle with mountains, for they are big and you are tiny. They were here before you. They'll be here after you.

Having just that extra sweatshirt on my first hike up Mount Washington was a mistake I didn't make again. But when you hike Mount Washington these days, hundreds of others are doing the same thing. If you get into trouble, it's only minutes before another hiker passes you and can offer assistance. The trails are crowded. But that's not the most frustrating part of the Mount Washington experience.

After spending many sweaty hours hauling yourself through trails, up rocks and boulders, and facing the elements along the way, the last push to the top is completely demoralizing. Imagine hauling yourself up the last rock and then looking up at a paved parking lot, glancing over to see an obnoxious woman in a mini-skirt and high heels jump out of a BMW and yell, "Look! I'm at the top! I'm at the top!"

There's a paved, well-maintained toll road and a cog railroad to take you to the summit with ease. Countless cars around New England sport bumper stickers that read: "This Car Climbed

Mount Washington." Meaning the summit views from New England's tallest peak are earned by anyone willing to endure the physical challenge of climbing it . . . or anyone with a car and a few bucks to pay the toll.

Not that its views aren't majestic. But I've just found other mountain peaks more satisfying when you realize that the only way to take in the view is to earn it through the climb. It's good to know that you can't drive anywhere near the top of any of the famed Seven Summits. Although I won't rule out trying to knock out one or two of those other six mountains at some point in my life, right now my focus is on Africa's Mount Kilimanjaro.

Part of this experience has been doing research and understanding this place at a cerebral level before I came here to drink it into my soul. Kilimanjaro is the tallest freestanding mountain in the world, meaning it's not part of a chain of mountains pushed skyward by tectonic plates colliding. This sucker is a volcano.

The mountain's earliest roots date back about three million years ago, when the Great Rift Valley was formed in eastern Africa. This mighty cut opened channels deep into the underworld, allowing magma (and whatever else dwells down there) an opening to push upward toward the heavens. About a million years ago, lava burst forth from the Great Rift Valley to form a volcano. The summit from this first event is called Shira today. It was active for about 250,000 years before she went quiet. But soon after, the region was rumbling again.

The next explosion occurred within Shira's caldera—pretty much exactly where our camp is right now—shortly after the first volcano became extinct. From this geological event, the Mawenzi peak formed, which can still be seen today. It looks like a traditional, cone-shaped volcano jutting out from atop a grand slope. I could see it from our hotel a few days ago.

Kilimanjaro saved its biggest and best act for last. About 460,000 years ago, an enormous eruption west of Mawenzi formed the tallest and most prominent summit, Kibo—it seems that the underworld wanted to push all the way up to the realm of God. Kibo is the summit most people envision when you say "Kilimanjaro." Further eruptions kept the mountain growing, and its flowing lava spilled all around the base, forming the saddle between Kibo and Mawenzi. Over the millennia, the mountain became taller and taller, reaching close to four miles into the sky until God allowed it to reach no farther; only then was Kili silenced. Her last volcanic activity dates back about two hundred years . . . which means, though dormant, Kibo is *not* extinct. This adds a further element of danger. I may make it to the summit, but if she wakes up, I'm dead.

The highest point of Kibo is Uhuru Peak. *Uhuru* means "freedom" in Swahili—and *that* is what's been calling me.

Precipitation typically doesn't fall at such high altitudes because the clouds and moisture are much lower. But snow reaches the top when southeast trade winds blow moisture in off the ocean and collide with the mountain, causing an enormous updraft that often leaves the top under a blanket of white snow. When the last Ice Age began, about 11,700 years ago, the Earth cooled. On Kilimanjaro, continuous moisture was driven up the mountain, where it fell as snow. Glaciers form when snow piles upon snow, and it remains cold enough year-round so that it doesn't melt. The snow compacts under its weight and forms dense ice. If the snow and cold continue, the glacier continues to grow. The process takes centuries.

Kili's glaciers are brilliant white, which helps sustain them because they reflect the sun's rays back upward. However, near the base, the dark rock absorbs the sun and heats up, slowly melting the foot of the glacier, making the ice unstable. The rest of the glacier is slowly disappearing through a process called *sublimation*, which occurs when glaciers are exposed to sunlight and dry air. Basically, the ice transforms from solid directly into gas and evaporates.

The glaciers and white snow on Kili's roof must have looked otherworldly to the people who dwelled here millennia ago, living their entire lives without seeing snow up close. The Chagga people first lived around the base of this great mountain. They were hunters and gatherers and found plenty of fresh water, roots, and animals to hunt in this fertile region. Their earliest religion centered on ancestor worship and a deity called Ruwa, who lived on the top of Kilimanjaro. Ruwa is an interesting god because he created neither the universe nor humans. Instead, Ruwa was involved in freeing humanity from some kind of prison, and then he had little more to do with us.

There is some debate over the exact meaning of the word *Kilimanjaro*, but there's no argument that it comes from the Chagga people. Missionary Johann Ludwig Krapf came to eastern Africa in 1846. He wrote that *Kilimanjaro* translates to "Mountain of Greatness," which sounds good. Another story says that when Europeans arrived here, they did their best to pronounce a KiChagga phrase that means "We failed to climb it," and assumed that was the name of the mountain. The most likely meaning is a bit more mundane. *Kilima* is the Swahili word for "mountain," and *njaro* is the KiChagga word for "whiteness": so "White

Mountain," which makes sense considering the glaciers and snow.

The Chagga people didn't have one single name for this mountain, which is surprising considering that it's the most prominent feature for many hundreds of miles. If you get lost, just look for the giant mountain and you'll find your way. The names of the peaks, though—Mawenzi and Kibo—do come from the KiChagga language. *Kimawenzi* means "having a broken top or summit," and *kipoo* means "snow."

On the Kenyan side of the mountain, the Maasai people called this place *Oldoinyo Oibor*, which means "White Mountain." And they referred to Kibo as *Ngaje Ngai*, or the "House of God." I'm reminded of the Native Americans of New Hampshire viewing their tallest mountain and reaching a similar conclusion: great mountain peaks hold great spirits. Hemingway makes that point in the introduction to his story "The Snows of Kilimanjaro." They believe that it's God's realm up there.

In August 1861, the Prussian baron Karl Klaus von der Decken and English geologist Richard Thornton made the first attempt to reach the highest summit, but they tapped out around 8,200 feet. In the coming decades, others tried and also failed. The first successful summit of Kilimanjaro (at least the first that was documented) was in 1889, by Hans Meyer and Ludwig Purtscheller. It was their third attempt at the climb. The pair established multiple camps with food and supplies so they could make more than one attempt at the summit if necessary.

In September of that year, the duo, along with their porters, had established a base camp as high up Kili as they could muster—they figured that this camp was about the same altitude as the summit of Mont Blanc in the Alps of Europe, which is 15,777 feet. For ten days, they lived at this camp, making attempts at the summit. Using axes and ropes, the men chipped and picked along the imposing face of the glaciers that guard the sacred summit of Kibo. At times, only clinging to their axes kept them from falling to their certain death.

On October 3, the two men chose a path that took them to the very top of the glaciers and gave them their first look at the summit. But they were exhausted and lacked the ability to finish the short ascent to the top. Down, but not out, they dragged themselves back to their base camp and rested for three days, acclimatizing and resting for another push. Three days after that, they tried the same route. Learning from previous missteps, they were able to ascend the glacier wall and reach the volcanic rim, elated to be the first men to accomplish this feat.

Meyer would write about the moment in his book *Across East African Glaciers: An Account of the First Ascent of Kilimanjaro*: "Taking out a small German flag, which I had brought with me for the purpose in my knapsack, I planted it on the weather-beaten lava summit with three ringing cheers, and in virtue of my right as its first discoverer christened this hitherto unknown and unnamed mountain peak—the loftiest spot in Africa and in the German Empire—Kaiser Wilhelm's Peak."

As if these Europeans had the right to name someone else's mountain . . .

Meyer continued: "Njaro, the guardian spirit of the mountain, seemed to take his conquest with a good grace, for neither snow nor tempest marred our triumphal invasion of his sanctuary. . . . It is a spectacle of imposing majesty and unapproachable grandeur, and the effect in our case was enhanced by the consciousness that we of all men were the first to gaze upon it. It was a never-to-be-forgotten experience." He then picked up a rock from the highest point they could measure to bring back as a gift for the German emperor. Purtscheller turned forty the day they reached the highest point of the volcanic rim. He was only two years younger than me. A reminder we can still do great things in our forties.

This mountain is also considered sacred to animals. The Chagga people tell a story of how the elephants around Kilimanjaro climb to the summit when it's their time to die. The legend states that the crater is filled with their bones and tusks, putting them out of reach of poachers. They claim that if you dare venture into the crater to see for yourself, and take even one piece of ivory, you'll be cursed forever.

While it's a great legend, we haven't heard reports of climbing groups getting passed by dying elephants . . . yet, as with any legend, there is truth to it. The elephants see this magnificent mountain just as we do. They must also feel some sense of awe. Skeleton bones from elephants have been found as high as the 15,000-foot mark on Kili. So some elephants did choose to lumber up this great mountain to die.

Dozens of human deaths have been documented on this mountain over the years. Some people have died from high-altitude illness, and others from rock falls, lightning strikes, or other mishaps. It's a sobering reminder that what I'm doing has proven fatal to some. Unlike the elephants, I didn't come here to die. Although sometimes it's good to remind myself that this place has been the last stop for others. Still, my mind drifts to what it must feel like to stand at the summit. Since 1889, countless people have successfully reached the top. I pray to be counted among them in the coming days. If God dwells atop Kibo, I hope to find that out.

Meyer and Purtscheller estimated that Kili's ice cap occupied about 12.5 square miles at the top. By 1912, another survey estimated that the ice had dwindled to 7.5 square miles. By 1953, a more accurate measurement placed the glaciers at 4.3 square miles, and a 2003 survey calculated their coverage at 1.5 square miles. These glaciers are going to disappear during my lifetime due to climate change. I'm fortunate to see them now, from the remains of Shira's extinct caldera.

As I sit here sizing up this mountain of greatness across Shira's plain before me, I'm sizing myself up at the same time. I'm feeling questions and doubts again. I'm okay now, but will I be tomorrow? The sun is dipping lower behind me, but it still warms me all over.

In Mr. Clark's English class in high school, we discussed how stories have themes like man versus man, man versus nature, and man versus himself. When I first made the decision to train for Kilimanjaro, I figured the theme was man versus nature. With a winter of hiking experience behind me, I now know it's not. When humans take on nature, they lose. Every. Single. Time. Nature can't be beaten. You may get your licks in, but in the end, you're going to be dust in the ground of nature.

Nor is this climb man versus man. I'm in competition with no other person out here. This is man versus himself. My body, my mind, my spirit. That's a battle that can be won. It may also be my greatest. Others have climbed Kilimanjaro, but not me. Not yet. If I succeed, I get to bring that home and keep it forever.

AS I PHOTOGRAPH AND FILM this mountain, I ponder the physical challenge I'm going through, but I also think about the spiritual aspects of this journey. I was raised Catholic. I went to church every week as a child out of obligation. As I got older, my church frequency slowed. By college, I was hardly going at all, and I harbored a lot of anger toward my religion (and really *all* religions, to be fair). I won't say I was ever an atheist, but I got close.

The reason I was never able to make the jump to atheism, ironically, is because of science first, and beauty second. I have been personally convinced of the existence of evolution. I don't think evolution is an affront to God—in fact, I think it makes God greater. I could grab a piece of paper right now and draw a clock face on the paper with the time reading 10:29—which is exactly the time as I type these words. My clock would be both perfect and accurate, *right now*. But in only a minute, my clock would be a little bit off. In twenty minutes, my clock would become a lot less useful. And in six hours, my clock is junk. (Go ahead and make the joke that my clock would still be correct twice per day.)

On the other hand, God is a clockmaker who knew the clock would need to change and built it to do so. I also believe the theory of the Big Bang holds a lot of credence. This is the idea that 13.7 billion years ago, there was an explosion that sent everything in our universe hurling outward at a tremendous speed. Scientists have theorized that all hydrogen atoms formed a few minutes after the explosion, once the universe had cooled just a bit. Given that matter and energy can't be created or destroyed, that means we are all truly eternal. This mountain, Kilimanjaro, was in those particles somewhere billions of years ago, and so was I, mixed with the molecules of this mountain and even of you, a little bit.

At one point, something came from nothing. For me, that requires a deity.

That's reason one why I believe in God. For reason two, I admit that my arguments are much less sound. Beauty. The fact that I can be stirred by a wide vista, the color of leaves in autumn, or this majestic mountain is something I can't quantify. When I look out at the plain in front of me, and Africa far beyond the mountain, and the summit above me, I see terrain that has indeed changed over time due to plate tectonics, volcanic activity, erosion, and other natural forces. But I can't help but see the brushstrokes of God too.

Right here, I have a gooey feeling deep inside me, like what I felt in church as a kid before I knew too much. I believe again. *This* is my church. Kilimanjaro is bringing me back to my own version of faith because it's brought me back to the mountains. Not for my job, not just for fun, but for my soul. My fat soul, which is toning up because of this journey.

The camera films, and I watch. Behind me, a white-necked crow scrounges around for any food we may have dropped. He's only a few feet from me, but he doesn't seem to care. It's obvious he's figured out that humans aren't a threat to him. He's seen us before, we're messy, and he can easily feed off of what we leave behind.

When the sun kisses the hills behind me, starting the night's slow fade to black, I head back to my tent to store my cameras, and then I make my way to dinner. Inside the yellow, hivelike mess tent, there's hot water for tea, hot chocolate, and coffee. And in the afternoon, they make us popcorn and set out platters of the stuff along with gingersnaps. We sit and chat about our lives, what we do, and some of the things we've seen so far. It's peaceful and leisurely.

For dinner, they bring us more hot soup, followed by spaghetti with meat sauce. I eat all of it and go back for seconds. Augustine joins us for the postdinner rundown on tomorrow's plan.

"Tomorrow, we start a bit different," Augustine says. "Some people in the group think we go too *pole pole* . . ."

I can tell he's struggling with this, because he wants to keep us all together.

"So tomorrow some of the group will go faster with another guide," he said. "And the rest will leave about thirty minutes later."

I'm thrilled at the notion of not hearing the complaining. That woman, Nancy, has become something of a pebble in my boot. It's annoying. It's easy to focus solely on the discomfort of that one little thing under my toe and miss the rest of the amazing world around me. The only options for dealing with a pebble in my boot is to stop, take the boot off, and remove the offending pebble; try my best to ignore the minor discomfort; or learn to live with it—allowing the pebble to hit the same spot under my toe over and over until I become indifferent to the annoyance. It seems that, at least for tomorrow, Augustine is pulling the pebble out of my boot for me.

Before leaving us for the evening, Augustine offers me a pro tip. "Try not to drink anything after six p.m.," he tells me. "Then you won't have to get up in the night to make pee."

Augustine is adamant about drinking three liters of water per day, but it should be done before six in the evening. This is good advice. Getting out of the tent in the cold darkness is a bitch. I learned that my first night.

Sunset at Shira 1 Camp. The clear skies soon give way to a starscape unlike any I've seen in my lifetime.

The sun is setting fast. Just a few minutes left of twilight, as colors fade from the world. The Scottish people call this time "the gloaming." There's magic in these transitional moments. The sun is leaving us until tomorrow. I hope it comes back. Some of the yellow tents already glow inside from lanterns. It's a cloudless sky above. A big sky, from this plateau. If I tilt my head back, there's nothing but sky.

As the last glow of light on the horizon disappears, I look up and stand in mouth-dropping awe. I've never seen so many stars. Not like this. There's Mars. It's so obvious by its orange glow, right there! I see the Southern Cross constellation, a sight only visible in the Southern Hemisphere, and one I haven't seen since my trip to Australia a few years ago. But the masterpiece of this celestial art gallery is the Milky Way galaxy—so clear as it runs straight up and down from the horizon. A sea of stars shining like diamonds through the clearest air I've ever breathed.

"Dude," is all Brian manages to say next to me. He dives for our tent to get his SLR camera and tripod.

When I was growing up in Connecticut, I used to lie on our back deck at night and look at the stars. If I focused just right and tuned out the trees and houses, I felt like I was floating in space among those stars. I'm that fourteen-year-old kid again, but now I'm standing tall among the stars—a man now. From where I'm standing, I see more stars than I ever imagined were out there. Everyone should see this. I thought I'd admired starry skies before, but I was mistaken. I'm seeing stars for the first time right now. This is what our ancestors saw millennia ago. I'm not sure there's any place in New England that's close to this heavenly evening view.

Without the sun, the temperature drops quickly. I'm shivering a little, but I'm not quite ready to look away. Brian finishes clicking his long-exposure night sky pictures as some of the lights within the tents around us extinguish. I head into the comforts of Tent 3. I placed the plastic case that holds my batteries, cameras, and phone into the bottom of my sleeping bag by my feet. I was warned by a photographer friend that cold weather will drain batteries—you need to keep them close to your body. It's cold enough here at Shira 1 that I take that precaution.

With the plastic case by my feet, I swallow two sleeping pills and nuzzle into my sleeping bag. I won't call my bedtime graceful, but it's an improvement from the night before. I'm not as uncomfortable as last night either, and soon I fade like the sun, knowing that Kilimanjaro and all those stars are outside keeping watch.

3 WEDNESDAY

SHIRA 1 CAMP TO SHIRA 2 CAMP

MY EYES CRACK OPEN with that "I can't sleep any longer" feeling. Like a meal when you're full, sleep has lost its appeal. I remember nothing between laying my head down last night and this moment of waking. A glorious feeling—thank you, sleeping pills!

It's just getting light outside, which means it's about six o'clock. Somewhere in the camp, people are walking around. It's in the distance, though. I exhale and see my breath. It's cold. I need to pee, but I'm not ready to leave my cocoon yet. I'm grateful to my sister, Sue, who bought me this sleeping bag for Christmas a few months ago. I make a mental note to thank her again when I get home.

Brian sighs and sits up. More stirring in the camp. I take a deep breath and unzip my bag. The cold slips into my bag alongside me, and I shiver awake. I search for my fleece jacket, feeling through my large dry bag until I find it. I reach around until I also find my fleece hat. Brian had all his morning clothes already set out so that he could slip them out of his bag and slide into them. Once again it's obvious I'm a hack camper, but I'm learning.

I emerge from the tent to see the mountain has no clouds on it at all. Crystal clear. Both the ground and our tent are covered with frost; I slept in below freezing conditions—another first for me. *Nice.* Maybe I can handle this camping thing. I can't imagine going home and planning the next time that I can be far from electricity, running water, showers, and toilets, but still, I'm handling this. I'm grateful for the new experience and gaining confidence that I'd last more than ten minutes after the zombie apocalypse.

I grab my cameras and head back to the far side of the camp to take pictures of the mighty summit. Every few minutes, a better photo opportunity arises out here. I continue to struggle between documenting and experiencing. Backlit by the sun, the summit is glowing, and the bold outline of Kilimanjaro against the pale blue morning sky is dramatic.

AFTER BREAKFAST and packing up our tents, I slather on sunblock and pop on my dorky sun hat. It's drab gray, wide-brimmed, with drawstrings to tie under my chin should the wind want to serve as the fashion police and rip this ugly thing from my head. But I'm wearing it for function, not fashion.

The first group sets off: the complainer, the coach, and another woman from the California team. Today's hike is across the plateau. It's only a slight incline most of the way—another walk in the park, though the landscape changes as we progress. Given our

The clouds on the horizon shifting from bright white to darker grays. When rain comes, I'll have the gear, but I won't welcome the muddy terrain.

slow pace, it's a comfortable trek. About an hour into the hike, I jog maybe twenty yards off the path to take a picture of our group hiking in a line. When I jog back to catch up, I find myself panting longer than I should. My head hurts slightly, a reminder that there's not as much air here, at 12,000 feet. I experience only the briefest flashback to my childhood and the anxiety of feeling those first wheezes of asthma, knowing it could get worse. *Pole pole.*

I grew up with asthma. Dog and cat fur would set it off, as would heavy dust. But damp or cold weather would too. I played soccer as a kid, and sometimes I would be limited to one quarter of the game, or just a few minutes of play at a time. I'd wheeze, my chest would heave, my mother would fret, and I felt like an invalid. I was different from the other kids. Sure, I wasn't the only one with asthma, but when I couldn't catch my breath as the others ran around, I felt weaker than my friends.

"You'll outgrow it," I was told. But at age twenty, I still had to take my inhaler, I still had medicine, and I *still* felt weaker than others. I'm not saying asthma is the reason I continue to feel like an outsider and weirdo, even today, but it did make a contribution to the cause. I've lived with asthma my whole life. I've noticed stress can also be a trigger for me.

In many ways, my asthma was a crutch. If I were struggling athletically, I could say, *Oh well, that's my asthma. I just can't run like other kids.* During soccer tryouts in high school, I was one of the last people to finish the long run that we did during captain's practice. I was huffing and puffing. The captains were about to make me run again when I pulled out my inhaler and took a puff. They saw that and pitied me, and they laid off.

My mother was always afraid. Every time I'd start to pant from exercise, she'd say, "You're going to have an asthma attack!" If an attack did strike, I'd be driven to the emergency room for shots of epinephrine. It happened enough that I felt the threat of the event hovering near me like a ghost. During these episodes, my breathing was so forced that my ribs would hurt for hours after an attack, but I never felt like my life was in danger.

For my mother, though, asthma was the Angel of Death, waiting for me around the next corner. I wasn't worried, but I couldn't help but feel her concern seep into my skin no matter how hard I tried to push it away and ignore it. I carried this well into my adult life. Yes, my asthma did get better, especially after I started running regularly, but it never completely went away. *Outgrow it, my ass.*

WHITE CLOUDS SKIM BY US on the trail. Augustine stops us for "flower-picking" and a water break. As some walk off to find a rock to pee behind, I look around. We're following a stream bed with just a tiny bit of water lazily moving through. I head down next to the stream and grab a photo very low to the ground that shows the stream with Kili in the distance.

"I'm smelling flowers," I tell Christine. That's been our code throughout training to stop and smell the roses. Not to forget that we're seeing and doing some incredible things. So I'm smelling flowers. Others are picking them. Kind of gross, if you think about it. So I don't.

The landscape constantly changes en route to Shira 2 Camp, though the summit mostly remains in view thanks to sunny skies.

I STARTED HIKING AFTER COLLEGE. I've hiked plenty of mountains around New England. One personality trait that's been exposed through this hobby of mine is how goal-oriented I can be. I often put my head down and speed-walk or climb until I get to the summit.

Three years before the Kili trip, I had the opportunity to hike Mount Washington alone. As I mentioned earlier, while it's never a good idea to hike without a partner, Mount Washington's trails are so heavily traveled that if I did fall and break my leg, I wouldn't be out there more than ten minutes before the next hiker came by.

On that solo hike, I hardly stopped along the ascent. Most people take an average of four hours to reach the summit, and I did it in just over three. I wasn't racing anyone; I just didn't want to stop. Also, I knew I had to get back down and then drive about forty-five minutes to the Mount Washington Hotel on the other side of the mountain for a conference. So I wasted no time either going up or down. By the time I checked into the hotel and took a shower, the entire lower half of my body felt like a rusted robot. Every step hurt. As more time passed, the pain only increased. Navigating staircases was brutal, and the few beers I chugged at the reception helped only slightly.

Moving at that rapid pace, I had put my body through unnecessary pain. Even worse, I had missed the glory of the journey. By keeping my head down, I had seen my feet, the dirt, and the rocks—the shit. That hike showed me how I sometimes move through life: focusing on the goal, the summit, the end of the project. And often missing a lot along the way.

Christine had said in some of our training hikes that she can be the same way. So on this hike, we vowed to remind each other to smell the flowers. There were times during training that she tapped my shoulder, pointed to a view, and simply said, "Flowers." I appreciated every reminder then, and I do now.

As for "picking flowers"—well, the term sounds pretty (and is meant to), but the reality is a challenge. It's pretty wide open here, so nearby boulders and bushes offer the only privacy for those who have to go. Vanessa from the California team heads behind a large rock to pick her own flower. Most of the women on this trip have brought a She-Wee; another popular brand is the Go Girl. It's basically a funnel that allows women to urinate standing up—pretty handy for rugged conditions.

A She-Wee mishap offers Vanessa discomfort, a story to tell, *and* a potential new online profile picture.

Vanessa is utilizing one of these right now . . . or rather, I would soon learn she's trying to.

"Oh my God, you guys," Vanessa calls out from behind the rock.

Her head pops above it. She's laughing hysterically.

"Something went horribly wrong with my She-Wee, and it spilled back into my underwear!"

We all laugh because she's laughing. But seriously, that sucks. The end result is equal to pissing your pants hours from the next camp.

"I'm really naked and afraid now!" she yells while holding her green, wet undies above her head.

"Wait!" I yell. "Hold that pose!" I raise my camera. She smiles big and waves her wet panties.

I click. "I have your new Facebook profile picture ready for you!" I yell back.

Vanessa comes out with her undies hanging off the back of her backpack to dry. This chick is hysterical. She marches on, mumbling about how the She-Wee didn't work right.

"I'm guessing it was user error," I said.

"No way!" she says.

The She-Wee is a plastic funnel, it's not like it has mechanical parts that malfunctioned. Then I reminded myself that I've had experience with a penis for more than forty years. I made my urination mistakes decades ago. She's on Day 2. I should give her a break.

Farther along, near a sign pointing the way to Shira 2 Camp, a huge boulder sits on the side of the trail asking to be scaled. Brian is the first to climb to the top and pose for a picture. With the summit in the distance behind him, it is a great shot. When he

The boulders on the Shira Plateau feel like a schoolyard jungle gym, begging to be climbed.

comes down, I'm next. The rock is dry and my boots get a good grip. I make my way to the top while others click away.

Christine is next, and after her photo op, as she climbs down, I notice that one of our guides, Steve, is waiting on the other side of the rock, ready to catch anyone who falls. These guys nearly have a heart attack every time one of us does something off the trail. I get that, though. They want to keep us safe and happy. If anyone is injured, it's bad PR.

Each day, my admiration for the guides grows. I've taken to calling our head guide, Augustine, *Mwalimu*, which means "teacher" in Swahili—something I remember from my college days. It's also a term of respect. He smiles and calls me *Mwanafunzi*, "student."

We're back on the trail. Always moving *pole pole*. Steve is leading us now. He takes a step, gently kicks the back of his heel with his other foot, then places that foot in front. He kicks the back of his other heel again. And so on. It's how he maintains the slow pace. It's slightly frustrating to go this slowly, but at the same time, I realize if I were in the lead, I would go too fast, my muscles would burn, and I would be toast the next day—just like my solo encounter with Mount Washington. At this pace, I have the opportunity to see and drink in everything and not burn out my body. For me, it is also an exercise in relinquishing control. I have to trust others and their experience.

I'm getting to know our guides as we walk and talk. Sunday, who leads the singing at the camps, is a guy I'd party with any day of the week. He tells me that he's been to the summit over two hundred times. That's over two hundred times more than me, so I default to his judgment on pacing.

During a lull in the conversation, Wilfred asks us if we've heard of Jamba Juice in the United States.

"Sure," some of us reply. Jamba Juice is a chain of fresh juice stores that are popular, especially on the West Coast. I've seen them in airports.

"*Jamba* means 'fart' in Swahili," Wilfred says.

Several of us laugh because we're completely immature.

"And you know the food taco?" Wilfred asks.

"Of course."

"*Tako* in Swahili means your butt," he says.

We're in hysterics now as we keep walking. And keep climbing our way up to Shira 2 Camp. Soon we walk into a misty gray cloud bank that's settled over our trail. Our visibility is limited to two hundred feet or so at times. There's odd comfort in miles of visibility—as if I'm safer knowing what's coming up far ahead. This cloud cover makes me feel more vulnerable and colder. The terrain turns otherworldly. It's mostly rocks and gravel, with a few strange trees called *Dendrosenecio kilimanjari* growing purposefully toward the sky. They look like spiky, short palms, almost like something out of a Dr. Seuss book. I expect the Lorax to jump out at any moment.

During our next "flower picking" break, I make my way back twenty or so yards to find a private spot among the bushes. After finding a tall enough bush to block the view, I take care of what I have to do. As I'm almost finished, I hear a loud hiss behind me. Mind you, I'm not quite done, and I don't know about you, but it's difficult to stop once you're going, but now I'm scared that there might be a *freakin' giant python right behind me* . . . and I just disturbed her nest or something.

These trees, *Dendrosenecio kilimanjari*, look like something out of Dr. Seuss. I keep waiting for the Lorax to jump out.

I piss as fast as I can and zip up while half-jogging back to the group. Then I see Jason about ten yards away. He was also picking a flower.

"Did you hear that hiss?!" I ask him, near panicked.

"Oh," he says. "That was me—I was just blowing my nose." What he meant was he launched a snot rocket. An air hanky. A gym teacher's Kleenex. I catch my breath. I snicker at myself, then walk back to the group. It's far too easy to imagine strange creatures in a strange land waiting to eat me—or parts of me.

Within the cloud, I don't have much sense of the landscape, other than that we're heading steadily up a slight incline. It's mid-afternoon when I walk into Shira 2 Camp. After signing the log book at the camp's shack, I make my way to Tent 3. My tent is familiar now, the way that a hotel room feels after I've stayed in it a few days. I know it's not home, but it is today. The plan is to unload our gear and sleeping bags, rest for an hour, and head farther up the mountain to acclimatize. Then we'll come back down before dinner.

Shira 2 Camp sits at 12,600 feet. For some perspective on just how high up I am right now, I remember the laws governing the Federal Aviation Administration and pilots, which I had researched before we left:

§ 135.89 Pilot requirements: Use of oxygen.

(a) *Unpressurized aircraft.* Each pilot of an unpressurized aircraft shall use oxygen continuously when flying

   (1) At altitudes above 10,000 feet through 12,000 feet Mean Sea Level (MSL) for that part of the flight at those altitudes that is of more than 30 minutes duration; and

   (2) Above 12,000 feet MSL.

SHIRA 2 CAMP

Elevation: 3,850 meters
above sea level
(about 12,600 feet)
Vegetation Zone: Moorland

FROM SHIRA 2 CAMP TO:
Baranco Camp: 10 km
Karanga Camp: 16 km
Barafu Camp: 20 km
Uhuru Peak: 25 km

In other words, if I were piloting an unpressurized aircraft right now, I'd be breaking the law. I don't overthink this point. I can breathe, and that's good enough for now. Our plan is to spend the entire night at this altitude and head even higher tomorrow.

I lie down in the tent, but I'm not tired enough for a nap, so I head out to sit on a rock outside to write in my journal and snap more pictures. Although each step I took today seems insignificant in and of itself, they all add up to one hell of a journey. I'm grateful that my feet have carried me this far. Not just up to Shira 2 Camp, but through decades of living, wandering, wondering, exploring, and learning. My feet have played their part.

There are a number of routes to the summit, and we're taking the Lemosho Route. It's the longest trail, but it's also the one where climbers have the most success (60 to 80 percent, depending on whom you ask), as the longer journey allows your body to adjust to the higher altitude more slowly. The other routes can get you to the summit in five, three, or even two days, but those present big-time breathing challenges to those unused to high elevations.

No one knows how altitude will affect you until you get there. There really aren't tests you can run (short of heading up a tall mountain). Each of us deals with the altitude a little differently. But the guides also have strategies to help us out. After our rest, Wilfred assembles us for the short hike farther up the trail. He tells us that it will help us acclimatize to the higher altitude and help us sleep.

I don't bring my backpack for this predinner hike—just my camera and a bottle of water. We're not going far, just up the hill to gain a few hundred feet in elevation. The higher you climb, the more stress it places on your body. As oxygen thins with increasing altitude, your body starts producing more red blood cells to make up for the depletion. By heading up a few hundred feet farther, we're tricking our body into producing even more red blood cells. Doing that will help us breathe easier during tonight's sleep.

That's the idea. Given that I have no other plans this afternoon, I'm on board. Since we're in a cloud, there isn't much landscape to see, but there are these funky, lava-formed outcrops. They make up a series of stone chambers maybe twenty feet tall, like ribs sticking out of a central spinal column. The rock is dark brown, with pits and rust-colored patches. It looks like it could have formed just a few decades ago, but in all likelihood, it was more like hundreds of thousands of years ago. It's just that there aren't many factors up here to weather or change the rock.

As we make our way up the mountain, we come across these stone chambers, left behind by ancient volcanic eruptions. Like the boulders on the Shira Plateau, their walls beg to be climbed.

These rocks have existed throughout the history of *Homo sapiens.* They have been around since our oldest ancestors walked the Earth. Had those ancestors found their way up here, they would have seen what I'm seeing right now. This land was never developed, never farmed; it's just as the volcano made it.

I stare at the inner part of these chambers without a roof and find myself drawn to climb them. Up I go. With so many footholds and handholds, it's an easy scramble to the top. I look down to see the rest of the team plodding along. This feels like a playground. A big, rock playground. I don't play in playgrounds as I used to—after all, I'm a grown-up. After my daughter was born, I enjoyed a renaissance of playing in parks and on swing sets, but that was for my child's benefit, not mine. But I just climbed this damn rock because it was here. Because I could. Because it was fun. Just for *me*.

I'M WINDED, unlike how I would be at sea level, but it's not so bad that I can't recover. I take my time climbing back down and rejoin the group. As we venture farther up, I get to say, yet again, that I'm standing at the highest elevation I've ever been. The clouds above and around us turn a darker, charcoal gray, and gentle rain spits at us. Just a sprinkle, but it's enough to make me zip up my rain shell and flip up the hood.

Wilfred says, "We can go back now. This is high enough." We've only been walking for a half-hour. "The higher elevation," he continues, "even a little bit, will help you sleep later tonight."

The trip back down is quicker. You don't have to go *pole pole* downhill. The rain puts a spring in my step, as I'd rather not get soaked out here. Still, it's light rain and the first we've seen so far on this trip, so I can't complain. Within twenty minutes, we're back at Shira 2 Camp and still have some time before dinner. Brian, Belinda, Vanessa, Christine, and I go into the mess tent for some popcorn and gingersnaps. We laugh a lot. The five of us have been hanging around together and formed our own little clique. We didn't intend to—it just happened.

When the conversation loses steam, I head outside to take more pictures. Maybe taking pictures isn't a distraction anymore, but rather a reason to find and examine parts of the world I haven't previously seen. I want to remember this. I want to record it in my brain and my camera. Although there are no overwhelming events today, I do have a greater sense that something profound is happening to me on this mountain. I recognize and honor the fact that I may not spot a defining moment as it's happening—that it may take the benefit of hindsight to see it. So I keep looking, keep making notes, and keep taking pictures.

At dinner, they serve us what I think is banana soup. I expect a sweet and savory combination, but instead it tastes more like a salty potato soup. When I bite down on one of the soft, white lumps, I'm sure it's a potato, but our waiter, Philbert, explains that they eat green plantains, and that's how they taste. No sweetness, but plenty of starch and calories. They also serve us rice and chicken.

After dinner, and another check of my vitals, I catch the last glimpse of waning sunlight outside. To the south, far down the valley, is Tanzania. I find it easier to brush my teeth and get ready for bed when there's still a little light out, so I grab my toothbrush and head for a rock formation to spit. I still don't like camping, but I don't dislike it, either. There's something primal about where I am and what I'm doing. I'm unplugging from my overly digital world back home.

I lie down in my sleeping bag and zip up against the quickly dropping temperatures. Tonight, there's no struggle between man and tent or sleeping bag. I'm learning. I'm also taking this time to reflect. Lying in my cozy sleeping bag, I feel guilt again. Not so much "rich white man's" guilt, as I did before, but guilt that climbing a mountain has to be one of the most frivolous endeavors in all of human history.

Sunset at Shira 2 Camp, offering a last daylight glimpse southwest into Tanzania.

FOR MOST OF EARLY human history, mountains were sacred places where gods dwelled; humans were strictly forbidden. Legends often have good reasons for existing. Climbing mountains is dangerous. You can die. Staying away from them is in your best survival interest. But still, they call to some of us.

Although humans have ventured up mountains for thousands of years, the concept of mountaineering as a sport has been around only since the mid-eighteenth century. It's no fluke that this sport was born during the Enlightenment era—a time where the Industrial Revolution was just getting started. A thousand years ago, no one had time to climb a mountain! People had to farm, hunt, gather, and live. They could do nothing else because otherwise, they would not have survived. Once towns grew into cities and farming became an industry, some people had the time to study and innovate and automate. Only then did humans have the luxury of even thinking about hobbies, let alone climbing a mountain.

Once our bellies were sated and we knew that food and shelter would be available, our species had time to turn our heads skyward, gaze at mountain peaks, and wonder what it would be like to stand on top of them and look out. Once we did that, once we ventured into the heavens to try and get a closer look at God, there was no turning back. A sport—a pastime, a passion—was born. And those who were the first to conquer the great mountains became heroes in the eyes of many.

George Mallory is a legend in mountaineering history. In the 1920s, he and his climbing partner, Andrew "Sandy" Irvine, attempted the first climb of Mount Everest—the world's highest peak. The pair took part in three expeditions to Everest, trying to assess the best route to the top. Before one of those famous expeditions, a newspaper reporter asked Mallory, "Why do you want to climb Mount Everest?" His reply, called the most famous three words in mountaineering, has been applied to both molehills and mountains ever since: "Because it's there." The funny thing is, Mallory's response was really an off-the-cuff remark. A dismissive statement because he probably thought the question was kind of stupid. It's funny how a simple throwaway can be so profound in hindsight.

Mallory and Irvine's final expedition to the world's tallest peak was in June 1924. They made their way up the mountain under treacherous conditions, the thinnest of air, and against all odds. Through a telescope at one of their lower camps, the men were spotted about 800 feet shy of Everest's 29,029-foot summit. And then . . . nothing. The telescope lost sight of them. The men weren't seen again. They never came back down. Their helpers, Sherpas, and guides were forced to pack up their camps and head down, knowing that there was no chance for either man to survive.

Mallory and Irvine's fates were unknown for seventy-five years. In 1999, an Everest expedition set out to find human remains on the mountain. Mallory's body was discovered right about where he was last spotted: 800 feet below the summit. It's unknown whether he failed to reach the top or if he made the summit and died on the way back down. The dreamer and optimist in me give Mallory the benefit of the doubt. I sleep better thinking that he made it but didn't quite get back down to tell us about it. Other climbers use Mallory's story as a lesson that there's no point in using all your energy to reach the top if you lack the strength to get back down and tell the tale. As Mark Inglis told me, reaching the summit is only half the journey. You still need to get down. Although Kilimanjaro is close to 10,000 feet shorter than Everest, people die on the roof of Africa as well. I don't want to be one of them.

This land is ancient. Tanzania is home to the earliest archeological discoveries of human settlements, in the Oduvai Gorge in the northern part of the country. Stone tools and fossils have been discovered in that area, which gave rise to the region's apt nickname: the Cradle of Mankind. Somewhere inside me, I feel that human history. I have a cosmic connection to the country through the very strands of my DNA. If I could trace my family tree back far enough, it would lead from there to here.

The average annual take-home salary for a person in Tanzania is 34,608,233 Tanzanian shillings, which is about $14,600. That average includes doctors, engineers, IT people, accountants, and other professionals, so at least half the country takes home less than that. Today, Moshi has a population of just north of 200,000 people, occupying twenty-three square miles. Its roots go back thousands of years, to when the Chagga, Maasai, and Pare people lived and hunted in northeastern Tanzania, but its modern history dates to the late nineteenth century.

In 1893, four years after Hans Meyer and Ludwig Purtscheller conquered Kilimanjaro, Germany established a military camp in Moshi, part of the colony that they called German East Africa. Other than owning one of the most majestic views on Earth, right in the shadow of Kilimanjaro, I can't imagine the strategic importance of Moshi to the Germans. But they must have had their reasons. Once the railroad came through in 1912, the town became more accessible to the outside world and grew as a result. After World War I, the Germans were replaced by the British, and this area served as a military outpost during World War II under the control of the Allied countries, and later the United Nations.

Throughout this colonial history, the locals went about their lives. Major roads joined the railroad in connecting the country to Moshi, leading it to take official town status in 1956. In 1961, the area known as Tanganyika merged with neighboring Zanzibar to form the free and independent nation of Tanzania. Since then, Moshi has continued its expansion, and it officially achieved city status in late 2016.

Moshi is considered one of Tanzania's cleanest cities. Most of the visitors to this municipality are here for Mount Kilimanjaro in one way or another. They come to see the mountain, climb it, or take in a safari in nearby Arusha National Park. There are murals of Kili in the streets of Moshi, I saw a scale model of the mountain on a street corner, and when the clouds part, Kibo stares down on these people like some objective deity. Here, Kilimanjaro is an industry. Although it's considered clean and mostly middle class, to my Western eyes, Moshi is a place of real poverty.

I saw that firsthand while walking the streets. I saw people selling used shoes on a blanket, and people wearing Gap and Old Navy T-shirts (but there's actually no Gap or Old Navy in Tanzania—I checked—these T-shirts are donated from other countries). I saw a man pedaling a bicycle that was propped on a platform and powered a spinning stone instead of a front wheel. He was sharpening a machete as sparks showered from the stone onto the street below. Walking on the sidewalk, I saw huge holes—four feet deep, and up to six feet wide—right there in the sidewalk. Any town in the United States would have a police officer standing guard, giant orange cones, yellow tape, and a work crew on each hole until it was filled up, so that people wouldn't trip on it and break their necks. The potential for lawsuits would be obvious in the United States. In Moshi, they simply expect you to watch where the hell you're walking.

Street vendors ran up to us at every corner trying to sell T-shirts, original artwork, bracelets, and other trinkets. Everyone here will take either the Tanzanian shilling or the US dollar. In Moshi, as a group of a dozen white people, we wouldn't have stood out any more if we had flashing neon above our heads. So far as I could see, we were the only white people on the crowded streets.

Our guides on the mountain were also our guides through the city. They herded us like cats through the streets. In town, I was struck by how vibrant the colors were. Pottery was sold on the side of the road, painted bright blue, orange, and lime-green. The

The colors of Moshi: pottery lining a market street .

Streetlife in Moshi. Vendors with their wares on blankets on the sidewalk, alongside carts of fruits and vegetables.

buildings were painted the brightest shades of primary colors, each one calling for more attention than the shack next to it. Fruit stands popped with reds, yellows, and greens—bananas, watermelons, and huge orange carrots. Stone-faced women in colorful African garb sold those fruits and vegetables on streetside stands. I wanted to photograph all of it, and I wasn't the only one.

"It's considered rude to take picture without first asking," Augustine told our group.

The reminder made me feel ashamed. It should have been inherent. We weren't at the damn zoo, taking pictures of flamingoes flinging crap at each other; this was a bustling urban center with human beings. Although it looked exotic to us, this was everyday life for the people of Moshi. I felt ugly for even considering reaching for my camera and taking someone's picture.

Still, the documentarian in me also struggled. I wanted people back home to see this and to feel what I felt. The dichotomy of such poverty and beauty. But then I found redemption for my self-disgust that Sunday afternoon. Ten of us paid a driver to take us to a place we'd heard about from Leukemia & Lymphoma Society groups who came here before us—the Amani Centre for Street Children. The ride was only about fifteen minutes, but it gave me a chance to see Moshi by road in the daylight. I saw cafés that looked like tin shacks, markets, more vendors, and housing that lacked doors and windows. The rusted metal of the houses was painted in bright yellows, greens, and blues—the popping colors in stark contrast to the rust underneath. Each building looked an average of about fifteen feet in width—the size of my living room. Billboards for Pepsi and Fanta soda were familiar, but plenty of other signs in Swahili were not.

"This is middle class," Augustine leaned over to tell me. There were places where conditions were much worse.

The Amani Centre was just off a main road and down a dirt road. The property was fenced in. When our minibus pulled up, a uniformed guard carrying a rifle opened the security gate for us. It was clear within minutes that we weren't on their schedule for the day, and they weren't quite sure what to do with us.

The Amani Centre provides food, shelter, and education to street children, and dozens of the kids it helps—mostly boys—came around to check us out. Some smiled and said hello (in English); others looked on with a kind of detached curiosity. They were wondering what we wanted—if we were there to gawk, to help, or what. They were just kids, like all kids, but some of the boys wore a distrustful look that could have come from being ground down too soon in life.

The director ushered us into a classroom where kids were practicing music on plastic recorders. She gave us a brief overview of how the organization takes in street kids, runaways, special needs children, and kids whose parents might be addicted to drugs or unable to care for them. We were touched, and the ten of us emptied our wallets after the presentation. It was a good opportunity to make an immediate difference.

Three children in the corner played "Twinkle, Twinkle, Little Star" for us on their recorders, and we applauded. The director then asked what we'd like to do while we were there.

"Can we play with them?" I said.

"Sure!"

We were brought behind the building to where the kids were assembling. There was a small, stone-circle amphitheater to my

Boys from the Amani Centre for Street Children playing us a song.

left, a grassy area to my right, and some covered pavilions with tables and chairs in the distance for outside picnics or classes. The whole scene felt awkward at first. A few bold and friendly kids approached to say hello, and I introduced myself.

"*Hujambo*," I said. "I'm Jeff."

I shook some hands. One young boy, about eight years old, was kicking a mostly flat soccer ball. It rolled away from him, and Belinda kicked it back to him. Pretty soon, there was more kicking back and forth. While we were slowly breaking through the awkwardness, another group arrived—a dozen or so American students who had arrived to volunteer. Judging from the happy hugs they were getting from the kids, this wasn't their first visit.

Behind the students, another teacher from the Amani Centre walked up, carrying a much nicer soccer ball, new and fully inflated. Soon a mob of us headed up a small hill toward the back of the property to where there were soccer goals and a dirt field. Both goals lacked nets. There was no grass to speak of, just dry, red, claylike dirt. No teams were picked, nothing was officially said, but the kids started running and dribbling the ball and the game began.

"The game is mostly street ball," one of the American students told me. "You try to get the ball and get it to a goal."

From our group, only Brian and I jumped into the game, along with two of our guides. Within a few minutes, the game naturally evolved into the kids against the adults. The awkwardness was gone. We were playing soccer now. No one cared who could speak English or Swahili; there was no malice, just a bunch of boys having fun. Some of the kids played barefoot, some wore flip-flops. (Flip-flops! How a kid can run in flip-flops is nothing short of superhuman.) Some had only one shoe, and most of these young boys were better than me at soccer, even though I was twice their size.

I looked around and saw that others in our group were playing with the girls down the hill, listening to them drum and sing. I was sweating, laughing, and playing soccer with these kids who wanted nothing more than to play. I made a few good plays—a block here, a takeaway there, a decent pass and cross—and it felt great. There was *joy*. I didn't feel out of place, as I had in the town. Yet I had to remind myself that soon I'd be heading back to

I played soccer my whole childhood, but I get smoked by a little kid in bare feet playing on dirt.

a nice hotel and moving on with my life, while these kids had this place to be, or else a potential hell back on the street.

After thirty minutes, we were told that it was time to wrap it up and head back. We high-fived the kids, and the director thanked us profusely for the donations. We signed their registry book and gave them our email addresses so we could keep in touch.

The dirt, sweat, and laughter cleansed me. I'd come to the Amani Centre and made a kind of offering of both money and time. I helped spread a few smiles as well. I was grateful for having this experience the very afternoon before embarking on the Kilimanjaro climb.

AS I LIE IN MY TENT at Shira 2 Camp, I think about that offering. My hope is that it's enough to appease God, who is waiting for me up there at the top. I pop in my earbuds and cue up Leonard Cohen on my iPod. I'm drifting off . . . "I heard there was a secret chord / That David played and it pleased the Lord / But you don't really care for music, do you?"

Hallelujah.

4 THURSDAY

SHIRA 2 CAMP TO BARANCO CAMP

A WIND CRACKLES at our tent like the sound of someone crumpling newspaper. It's not a gale force, just enough to wake me. Lying here in my sleeping bag, I'm not missing the shower as much as I thought. It helps that it's only been a few days, combined with cool temperatures and the *pole pole* pace that have helped to keep my sweat factor down.

I pull myself out of my sleeping bag, the same awkward rebirth as yesterday, but at least I have set the day's clothes out the night before so I can slide them on without facing the chill. Coming out of my tent, I gaze first to my right and notice a sea of clouds in the valley below. I've only seen a view like this from an airplane. It's beautiful. The clouds go on forever. It's like standing by an open ocean of white.

The summit of Kibo is clear once again. Like yesterday, there's a glow around its outline as the sun rises on the other side.

This morning I step out of my tent at Shira 2 Camp to a sea of clouds below me.

I continue clicking pictures and shooting video. I snap a shot just as the sun breaks over the northern edge of the summit.

Philbert brings around hot water and coffee cups.

"*Nataka chai*," I say. *I want tea*—I recall the phrase from my Swahili days. He smiles, pleased that I know a bit more Swahili than the average American. The warm cup, with a spoonful of cane sugar and Kilimanjaro brand tea, is welcome. I sip the tea and stare at Kibo—still in the distance, but noticeably closer than yesterday. It feels attainable from here.

Eating breakfast, checking our vitals, and packing up are routine now. So is my morning constitutional on the squatty potty. Some in our group have the runs, while others are bound up like Boston rush hour traffic. I don't take my regularity for granted. Nor do I brag about it. It's funny how open we are about things usually so private. Because out here on the mountain, it's a pretty big part of your day.

I strap into my backpack; I'm getting into the groove of this camping thing. I'm eager to start walking. We're going to new heights—all the way up to the Lava Tower, at around 15,000 feet, before heading back down to 13,000 feet at Baranco Camp. We're circumnavigating the southern side of the mountain above the tree line and following the terrain. The higher elevation of Lava Tower will also help us acclimatize.

Our sojourn begins on the same path that Wilfred took us on yesterday afternoon to acclimatize. *Pole pole* we go. The weather

Sunrise cracking the summit of Kibo, signaling time for breakfast, packing up, and moving out to the next camp.

is clear. The temperature is brisk. No frost this morning, so I'm guessing that the temperature is in the mid-forties. My body isn't sore right now; I have my training to thank for that. Exercising is a lot like my writing life. When I do it all the time, I'm better at it, I can go longer, and it flows, even if I'm not in the mood.

In my writing life, I'm at my most prolific when I'm juggling multiple projects at once. The words come easily. I can take a day off, even two, but I start to feel it when I start back up again after too many days of not writing. Exercising works the same way. I'm now in better shape than I was in high school. I'm writing more now than I have in my entire career.

I have put my faith in our guides, in my training, in me, in God, in the universe. My only job is to keep walking and climbing. Put one foot in front of the other. I don't think about the summit day two days from now, and I don't think about what phone calls or emails might be waiting for me at home, or even my family back in New England. I trust that those things are okay. My only concern is taking my next step. Being this unplugged from the world offers me a peace that I haven't experienced in years.

Earlier this month, I came across something online called "National Day of Unplugging." It's typically held the first Friday of March, and it consists of getting through twenty-four hours without using technology. I laughed when I first read about the idea. Then the gravity of the times I live in hit me. The more "connected" I've been through email, social media, text messages, and phone calls, the more disconnected I've felt from people. Obviously I'm not the only person who feels this way because an entire group has formed to encourage us to put down our smartphones for one day a year. I admit that I did not partake in the National Day of Unplugging this year. But I'm making up for it right now on Kilimanjaro.

I'm unplugged because I have no other choice. And it's having a positive effect. Looking back to the first day of the hike, I see now that I was dealing with some underlying tension. I chalked it up to anxiety at starting this epic journey, but at least part of that anxiety was knowing that I couldn't call, email, or text anyone, and they couldn't reach me either. After three days of being unplugged, that anxiety is melting away. I'm grounded to my home planet again with each new step. My social network consists of some pretty amazing people who are hiking with me, as well as the ambassadors of Tanzania who are quickly becoming *rafiki*. Friends.

I take comfort in so much newfound simplicity. My next step is my only worry. You climb a mountain the same way that you write a book. A book is written one word at a time. Words form sentences, then paragraphs, then pages, then chapters, and eventually you end up with a tome. If you think about writing a book as a whole, it's easy to be intimidated. This mountain is the same way. I focus only on the next step. That's my one concern. And it's a legitimate concern; as we gain more elevation, taking the next step is not as easy as it had been a few thousand feet earlier.

The landscape is changing again. Everything is turning reddish-brown. It's like I'm on Mars. I'm on a hill with scattered boulders and a few bushes about waist-high, surrounded by clouds. The trail is worn, defined by the countless footsteps of pilgrims who have come before me. It's a path in the sandy dirt, but a slightly different color from the dirt a few feet away.

The sobering plaque for Ian McKeever.

As we near the top of a long incline, a shiny, square stone resting on a nearby rock attracts my attention. It reads:

IN MEMORY OF

Ian McKeever

(1970–2013)

Who inspired so many to reach their own goals
and achieve their own summits

"Attitude Before Altitude"

Around the stone, people have placed various rocks, as well as dead flowers that had been picked a little farther down the mountain and been left there. The gravity of the event hits me. Someone died here. Right here. Ian was only one year older than I am now when he died. Right. Here. I know we're high up, but I can't imagine the altitude was enough to take a life at this point. Mark explains that Ian was struck by lightning. *Lightning* . . . That's an element of danger I hadn't considered until this moment.

I look again at the clouds floating all around us. Some are white; others have a touch of gray to them. If an electrical storm whips up, what would I do? I have plenty of metal on me, between my hiking poles, backpack, and camera gear. If lightning zapped around me, the only thing I could do is drop my pack and hide behind a rock.

We keep moving, but I keep an eye on those clouds. I don't trust them as I did farther down. Yet the clouds today don't seem angry about our presence; they allow us to pass through without incident. Farther up, a valley opens before me. It's otherworldly: brown, sandy, rocky. It's like the valley in *Star Wars* where the Jawas rolled up on C-3PO and R2-D2.

"These aren't the droids you're looking for," I say to Mark.

He looks at me, puzzled.

"Move along," I say.

He shrugs and walks ahead. Maybe it's the altitude . . . or maybe . . . just maybe . . . this experience has given me the powers of the Jedi mind trick.

THIS *FEELS* LIKE A MOUNTAIN AGAIN, with big rocks and steep inclines above me. I look to my left and see a slight, dusty trail leading down through the valley and up the next ridge. Our guides tell us that we'll stop for lunch at the top of that ridge. It doesn't look like much of a distance, but it takes us over an hour to get there. I plod along. I estimate we're at around 14,000 feet in elevation right now. As we climb the ridge, a cloud moves in and lowers the visibility and temperature. But as soon as it arrives, it moves out again. And once again I see the valley, but this time from the other side.

When we reach our lunch spot, I'm ready for a break, but I still have this inherent excitement. My body isn't tired at all. I eat with gusto—and gratitude, an emotion that's becoming more prevalent each day on this mountain. I've said *asante sana* (thank you) more times in a day than I have in a month at home. I make a mental note to change that. I have plenty to be grateful for at home. President John F. Kennedy once said, "As we express our gratitude, we must never forget that the highest appreciation is not to utter words, but to live by them." I'm reminded to move beyond the expression. I can find gratitude in each step I take.

Post-lunch, we start up another big hill toward Lava Tower Camp. I try saying "thank you" in my head with each step. Like a meditative chant. Then I switch to *asante* and notice that my mood lifts. It sounds corny, but I understand the expression "song in my heart." I feel good on the inside as I walk toward our objective in the distance. Maybe it's the *s* sound in *asante* that works like an exhale with each step, or the way that the Swahili word feels more lyrical. I don't care why, really. *Asante* feels right. So I go with the mantra without question.

Although Lava Tower is a camp, we won't be staying there tonight. It's just a rest area for us. The camp is aptly named. The tower is visible from our starting point and looks like a large column of thrust shot into the air and flash frozen, with its top broken off into a plateau high above.

The Lava Tower Camp sits at 15,100 feet in elevation. Once again, the highest elevation . . . you get it. The lunch break and my gratitude mantra have energized me and made me ready for

As we gain elevation, the landscape turns otherworldly. On the approach to Lava Tower, I expect Jawas, C-3PO, and R2-D2 to show up.

the next leg of the journey. While climbing the long hill toward Lava Tower, I start singing, as I'm prone to do on these things. This time it's "Wannabe," by the Spice Girls.

"If you wanna be my lover, you gotta get with my friends . . ." Vanessa jumps in, and then we start dancing in line. After the first chorus, "I really really really wanna zigga zig ahh," both of us are huffing and puffing like we just completed a sprint. I stop and hunch over, hands on my knees, trying to catch my breath.

"Dear God, that was stupid," I say. Huffing. Puffing.

"Yeah," Vanessa exhales.

Just thirty seconds of singing and a little booty shaking, and I might pass out. It takes me close to two minutes of very slow walking to catch my breath, and we're still well below Lava Tower.

In those two minutes, Vanessa and I have fallen behind the group. Maybe by only a hundred feet, but still. Although I've experienced shortness of breath on this trip at times, this is new.

When I exert myself at sea level, say a sprint across a football field, I can catch my breath in a matter of seconds. Stop running, a few deep breaths, and soon I'm back to normal. Singing the freakin' Spice Girls isn't exactly sprinting on a football field, and now I have a headache and my heart rate has accelerated due to the desperate need to get enough oxygen back into my bloodstream.

Although I'd been told dealing with altitude is exponentially harder as you climb above 10,000 feet, now I understand what that means. We're probably at around 14,500 feet when I pulled my Spice Girls antics, and now it feels like a slightly dangerous moment for spontaneous karaoke. *The summit is 5,000 feet higher than this.* The summit of Mount Whitney in the Sierra Nevada mountain range of California is the tallest mountain in the continental United States, at 14,494 feet. I'm standing as high as that mountaintop right now.

When we reach Lava Tower Camp, we take a water and "flower picking" break. Although I'm standing still, I'm still huffing and puffing to get enough air. Jason walks up from behind us. He looks pale.

"Are you okay?" I ask him.

"Yeah," he pants. "I'll be okay."

I trust he knows his own body and limits, but he doesn't look too good.

At 15,000 feet, there's about half the oxygen available at sea level. However you're breathing right now while reading this (unless, *yanno*, you're reading this at Lava Tower), you need to

LAVA TOWER CAMP

Elevation 4,600 m
(15,100 feet)
Vegetation zone: Alpine Desert

FROM LAVA TOWER CAMP TO:
Arrow Glacier Camp: 1 km
Baranco Camp: 3 km
Karanga Camp: 9 km
Barafu Camp: 13 km
Uhuru Peak: 18 km

breathe twice as deeply at this elevation to get the air you need. You want to know what that feels like? Go grab a drinking straw and breathe through that. Now go for a short jog while breathing through just that straw.

Countless asthma attack visions from my childhood flood through me. Blowing all the way out and inhaling as deeply as I can to get enough oxygen into my constricted airways. The panic of not being able to breathe only making it worse. The memory of my mother fretting as I wheeze through my breathing. Of her telling me I shouldn't play soccer because I have asthma. Of feeling weaker than the other kids, and eventually adopting asthma as my own crutch to avoid big physical challenges.

I tell myself that my airways aren't constricted right now. There's just less air to breathe. I close my eyes a moment and calm my nerves. Resting. My heart rate slows, and my breathing comes back to something close to normal.

According to the tiny thermometer on my backpack, the temperature is somewhere in the low forties. When the wind whips, it feels colder, and when the clouds part and the sun shines, it feels at least ten degrees warmer. But my layers of Techwick and fleece keep me comfortable. I've gotten pretty good at layering. The last thing I want is to sweat too much, but hiking while cold is just uncomfortable.

After snapping a few pictures at Lava Tower and taking a potty break and a drink of water, we're on our way again. As the landscape turns more challenging, I focus on breath and steps. It's the most in-the-moment living I've experienced in my adult life so far. Breathe. Step. Step. *Asante*. Breathe. Step. Step. *Thank you.* I feel the rhythm of my walking with my breath and the natural rhythm of the world around me. Maybe I'm just an American kid raised on movies, but when I think of Africa, I hear a drumbeat. It's primal. Like a deep heartbeat. Although there's no music, I hear it right now, somewhere deep inside.

From the Lava Tower, we start down a steep hill on the trail to the next camp. With each few hundred feet in elevation down into the valley, breathing is noticeably easier. We're heading to the Baranco Camp, three kilometers away. Halfway down the hill, I look up as the clouds pass by the summit to my left and some glaciers become visible again. They look so close! I'm struck by the scene, by this instant. I turn to Christine and say, "Christine, look! Have a moment with me." I put my arm around her shoulder.

She looks, and gulps. She's holding back tears, and pushes them down successfully. I'm surprised and not surprised at her reaction. For months, we've been reminding each other to stop and smell the roses on our hikes. It's one big fucking rose up here. A thousand Valentine's Day bouquets. The emotion of it catches us both. We're closing in on the goal. Circling the summit to eventually come up from the east, like we're prey and Kibo is our quarry. Although considering how outmatched we are, I know this analogy is ridiculous. Kibo could crush me with a sneeze.

As we make our way down to the bottom of the valley, we cross a small stream. All of the water flowing through here is meltwater from the glaciers above. Thousands of years of history are literally melting away as I step over the stream. This water flows from ice that's been up here for almost 12,000 years—since

Thousands of years of glacial history in gentle meltwater streams.

before the time of the pharaohs in Egypt, long before Jesus of Nazareth, and many millennia before I was born. Given how fast these glaciers are disappearing due to global warming, I'm fortunate to see them right now.

Down one hill, and up another. *Pole pole* we go. We crest the next hill and lumber on down the next valley. Since Wilfred told us that *taco* is pronounced exactly like the word *tako* in Swahili, we can't stop saying *tako*. Weary from the walk, Belinda calls out that we should be called Team Tako. *Boy, did that stick quick*. I laugh, Wilfred laughs. Soon we shout it across the valley, "Team Tako!"

Team Butt seems about right because at this point, some of us are falling on our *takos*. Nothing tragic, but tired legs and wobbly ankles mean sometimes you land on your *tako*. We're making our way down the final valley into Baranco Camp, which lies ahead of us. My legs are getting wobbly. It's a familiar feeling that I've had on the descent after long days on other mountains. Going downhill is always more difficult. Uphill is all muscle. If you get tired, rest. Downhill is all impact on your knees, ankles, and other joints.

We're close to camp—just a few hundred yards away. I'm looking ahead, I step down one rock, misstep, and feel myself falling backward. I throw my weight forward and jam my other leg down and slightly behind me in an effort to regain my balance. It works, I don't fall, but it comes at a price—I just pulled the quad muscle on my left leg. I feel the initial punch of a muscle sprain, I stand up again, and now pain shoots down my left leg in waves.

I'm both angry at myself and panicked. Memories of my training hike on Mount Monadnock in southern New Hampshire, four weeks earlier, come flooding back. We were coming down from the summit and had just passed the intersection of the White Cross and White Dot trails on Monadnock. I saw a cascade of solid ice over two big steps of rock on the trail in front of me. The ice covered everything, and there was no obvious way around without heading back and blazing a trail through the woods—something you're not supposed to do.

I walked to the edge and investigated going straight over the ice. My metal microspikes on my boots had held me so far, so I was mindful to give them a good stomp to dig into the ice before stepping. I stomped, then leaned forward to plant my other foot. I knew instantly that I had a problem. My first foot had never gripped the solid ice, and now I was sliding. It didn't matter what I did with my second foot now because I was going down.

This wasn't like falling in snow, where I know to relax my body. This was solid ice and rock. I tried to catch myself, or at least keep from sliding over the edge. The ice and earth slammed into my left arm and left upper thigh. I slid feet first. There was a rushing sound, a grinding sound, a *whoosh*, another bump, then awful silence for a moment that told me I was airborne as I cleared the first edge. A painful *thud* as I hit the second with my leg as if it were a stairstep, and then I saw a tree coming fast. I put my foot out to stop myself on the tree, and then it was over. I was motionless. The entire ordeal couldn't have taken more than two or three seconds, but time had slowed for me. My body was calculating every possible scenario and variable. Do I grab for something? Try and plant my pole? Try to dig a foot in? In the end, it was a tree that ended my fall.

Once I stopped moving, blinding pain shot from my left forearm. I was sure it was broken. I had pain elsewhere, but the pain in my forearm commanded the most attention. I tried to push myself up with my right arm. My vision blurred. My brain ran through a diagnostic check. I didn't feel any pain in my head, so I didn't think I'd hit my head. I pushed myself up on to my right hand and two knees, but I couldn't put my left arm down. I got myself into a kneeling position and held my injured arm like a baby. I was dizzy and nauseated. The frozen world around me was moving from blurred to focus, blurred to focus.

"I need a minute," I said to Sherpa Tom, once he caught up to me.

I stood up to "walk it off," but I soon realized I couldn't stay standing. I stumbled over to a tree stump a few feet away and sat down. I wiggled the fingers on my left hand and took that as a good sign. I bent my wrist as well, and that was working. I sat in the sunlight hitting Monadnock and found myself yawning. I could have gone to sleep right there. I yawned again. I told the group that they could go ahead and I'd catch up, but they didn't leave me. There was a dull ache in the back part of my upper left thigh, but I could tell that was just a bruise. Besides, I have plenty of meat on that bone. My focus was my arm. There just isn't much between your radius and ulna and the world.

"I'd know if this was broken, right?" I asked Sherpa Tom.

"Probably," he said.

I opened and flexed my arm, and then rotated it. I bent my wrist open and shut. I felt some dull pain when I moved, but that's all. I took all of that as more good signs. If my arm was broken, I had just lost Kilimanjaro. It would mean weeks in a cast, and there was no way that a doctor would clear me for the trip.

By the time I got home from Monadnock, I was growing confident that my arm was not broken, but the skin had split from the impact. There were blood and bruises, and a good lesson learned. I had time to heal, and I learned not to place blind trust in my gear. Microspikes aren't perfect. Nothing is. I also learned that near the end of the day is when I'm most likely to get hurt. My coordination isn't as good and my muscles are tired. I have to remember to rest on the descent too.

SHIT! I say quietly to myself. I'm pissed for not remembering the lesson of Monadnock until falling here. I step forward with a limp, trying to gauge how bad this is. I can still walk, but there's pain with each step. Sometimes a pulled muscle takes a few minutes to give you the full brunt of its fury; other times you can walk it off. I keep walking gingerly and wait to see which kind of pull this will be.

I wish I had simply fallen on my *tako*. It wouldn't have been a big deal at all. In saving my fall, I pulled a muscle, whereas my ass would have only been bruised slightly. I'm asking my leg if the summit is now in jeopardy for me. But my leg doesn't answer. I keep walking. The pain doesn't get worse. It's a dull ache. I take that as a good sign. We're close to camp, and I'm grateful this happened at this point. I'll be able to rest just ahead.

When we arrive at camp, there's something new: other campers. For the first time, we run into other groups. Ours is the largest, but still there are other camps set up here, with other groups of climbers from all over the world.

This place is called Baranco Camp because it sits in the shadow of the Baranco Wall, which looms about a hundred yards to my left. I also see a helicopter landing pad for emergency evacuations on the hillside to my right—another reminder that this can be a dangerous place. Tomorrow, our task is to climb the formidable Wall. But that's tomorrow; I'll worry about that then.

I'm told that there's a chance of getting a cell signal over by the sign-in hut. If there are no clouds and you can see the city of Moshi, far below to the southeast, it's a possibility. I walk over with my phone out like it's some kind of metal detector. I know the joys of unplugging from the world, but the allure of hearing that my family back home is okay, and telling them that I'm also okay, outweighs my newly acquired enlightened view of technology.

From above the clouds, I can see most of the city of Moshi, miles to the southeast. It looks the way that a town does when you're approaching an airport from the sky. I can't see any roads, cars, or people, just the buildings in some far-off pile. Two bars spring up in the upper-left corner of my phone. I text my wife that I'm at Baranco Camp and feeling good. She texts back right away. She's home, so I call her. I know it's $2.99 per minute for this call, but I haven't spoken to her since Sunday. She picks up and we can hear each other. She starts to cry. Not an ugly, sobbing cry, just happy tears that we can communicate, even if only for a minute.

"I got this," I tell her. She laughs. I ask how our daughter is doing, how she's doing, and I'm told everything is fine. I take comfort. While we're talking, Nancy the complainer is lurking around, also looking for a cell signal. It's just the two of us in this area right now, and she's talking loud—I assume so I'll hear her.

"How do you have a signal?" she says. "I don't have a signal, maybe if I stand right where you are, I can't get a signal . . ." All while I'm trying to talk to home. I take a deep breath and work to hold in my fury. This woman is under my skin. It takes all I have not to put the phone down and put her in her place right now. I'm lucky to get a signal to my family; it's foreign to me how she could consider this is a good time to pester me to help her.

"This place is amazing!" I tell Megan. "I'm doing great and feeling great. I really got this."

I don't mention my leg. I can hear the smile in her voice, and I'm reassured that things at home are all right. I tell her I'll text or call any possible chance I get, and that silence means everything is fine.

"I love you," I tell her. "And thank you for all of this."

I return to my tent and plug my phone into the external battery I brought with me. I have spare camera batteries, but my phone can only be charged twice off of this portable battery. So I use my phone sparingly for photographs and keep it turned off most of the time.

With my phone charging, I head to the mess tent for dinner, still contending with a sore leg. Shannon from California gives me some ibuprofen. We check our vitals, we eat, and then Augustine explains the plan for tomorrow in his gentle, quiet voice.

"Tomorrow we going up the Baranco Wall," he said. "It's 843 feet up from the canyon where we sleep tonight."

The Wall looks intimidating from outside the mess tent. I've heard from other groups that have already made the journey that it's the toughest climbing day so far. Still, I'll leave tomorrow's challenges for tomorrow.

It's colder here at Baranco Camp. Before zipping up for the night, I pull out some of the photos I brought with me for the summit. I have a picture of my brother-in-law, Chris, a picture of Chris and my nephew Henri together, and a photo of my wife and daughter holding our pet parakeet, Nimbus. I even brought a class photo from my daughter's school because I told her teacher that I'd take them all to the top. I hope I don't let them down.

I zip my sleeping bag all the way around my head so only my face is exposed. My left leg's dull ache reminds me it's there. I ask it to heal tonight.

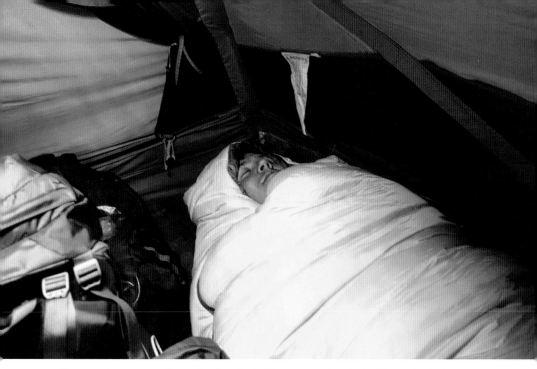

My zero-degree-rated sleeping bag feels like a cozy ski parka inside our tent at Baranco Camp.

5 FRIDAY

BARANCO CAMP TO KARANGA CAMP

I'M GETTING BETTER AT SLEEPING. Although I've had decades of practice in a bed, sleeping in a tent on a rock is still new to me. When I open my eyes, the familiar, grayish hue of the tent indicates it's getting light outside. My lower back isn't hurting, as it did after the first night in here. I'm learning to switch positions in my sleep and to surrender to the exhaustion that comes at the end of each day.

My main concern is the quad on my left leg. I run through my self-diagnostics of wiggling toes and fingers, slightly bending to the left and then the right within my sleeping bag, extending my legs and flexing and relaxing my muscles. So far, so good. Time for the real test. After pulling on the clothes I set out the night before, I rise from the tent and put weight on my left leg. It feels okay. Only the dullest of aches. I walk. Still good. My concerns fade. This trip ain't over for me yet.

I awaken to the summit looking closer than ever. Our route will have us coming around the volcanic rim to approach the summit from the east.

When I turn around, I'm greeted by the summit. It's the closest it's looked so far. Right up there, above that cliff behind me. Our route doesn't take us that way, though; we'll be circumventing the steep southern face of the summit and going up from the east near the top, but right now, it looks like Kibo is within my grasp.

At breakfast, Christine reminds me to take two more ibuprofens. I do, even though the soreness in my thigh is mostly gone. Today is going to be a short day—just four to five hours to Karanga Camp. *Hakuna matata*. But first, the Baranco Wall. After strapping on my pack and gear, I head east with the group, toward the Wall. The sun is rising from the other side of the Wall, so our entire camp is in shadow. It's colder here—maybe the low forties—but again we have clear skies above.

We're in a kind of canyon, with the summit high above the cliffs to the north and the route that we came in off to the west. Off of a sheer face and miles away to the south lies Moshi, while to our east, all 843 vertical feet of the Baranco Wall sits like some kind of ancient, massive stone guardian. When we arrived yesterday, the Wall looked as if it shot straight up. Today, as we get closer, I can see that the Baranco Wall isn't sheer, though it certainly is steep. The trail switches back and forth in a zigzag along the wall, so it's like climbing an eighty-four-story building taking the stairs—but there are no railings here. Our guides are nervous because a misstep could be fatal. Up to this point, a wrong step meant that you landed on your *tako*. But now you could go tumbling hundreds of feet down to a rocky grave.

Within the first few yards up the narrow, steep, rocky trail, I fall in love with the Baranco Wall. This feels like parts of Mount Washington, or even Mount Monadnock, back home. This feels like climbing a mountain! I'm wearing thin, fleece gloves to keep my hands warm, but I take them off and zip them into my pockets. I need my hands here. I like to feel the rock against my fingers. My skin grips better than my gloved hands would.

Big rocks and boulders are set along the route above me. I'm pulling myself up with my hands and arms, and hugging a rock face to get around a narrow part of the path. As the sun makes its way over the Wall, I warm up. I'm only wearing a long-sleeved Techwick shirt and my fleece. When the sun hits, I unzip the fleece. This type of climbing is more rigorous than hiking along a trail. I'm building up a little sweat.

The Baranco Wall is the most dangerous part of the journey, with spots where a fall would be fatal.

Some people are using hiking poles, but mine are strapped to my pack. I don't want to have anything between my body and the rocks. Parts of the trail are a few feet wide and easy to move along single file. Other sections involve hauling yourself up the rock face.

Our guides are specific about where to place each foot, which is disappointing. When I encounter a rocky wall back home, most of the fun of climbing is figuring out your route. Deciding where to put your own hands and feet to get to the top. There are a million ways to climb even a short wall. No two people will ever ascend the same way, touching all the same handholds and footholds. The guides are grabbing some of the people in our group by the arms to help them up. I wave them off.

I'm in my element here. I start finding my own paths up and around. I'm never far from the group, and soon our guides seem comfortable that I'm comfortable, and they focus on the others.

The ascent takes us about an hour. As I pull myself up the last stretch, I sigh, and I'm actually a little bummed that the Baranco Wall is over so soon. The rock-climbing portion of our day is now done. But the view . . .

Far below us, the Baranco Camp now sits empty. To my left, Tanzania is covered by a blanket of puffy clouds that allows me to peek through in places and see the green farmlands far off in the distance. Yet the sun shines brightly on us. Right here, right now, I'm at the gates of heaven. Just me and the mountain. I'm part of the sky, and yet I can feel a connection to the Earth.

The Baranco Wall is over too soon—dangerous, but the most fun, scaling its rocks and crags.

We walk over to a small plateau to take a snack and water break (and pick a flower, if the spirit moves you). A thick cloud moves around us, obscuring everything except a few dozen feet of visibility. The scene is dramatic, as if my fellow hikers and the guides were standing on a blank sheet of paper, with no other color or context around us. We're all silhouettes, shadows of what we were below.

Whether we hike out of the cloud or the cloud moves along on its own, I'm not sure. Likely it's both. The landscape ahead is brown and dusty and looks desolate and bleak, but I don't feel isolation or remoteness. This is the path I must take to get to where I'm going. I watch the next step, then the next, then the next. The summit isn't today's challenge, so I'm not giving it much thought other than passing admiration when the clouds part enough to offer me a glimpse of it. This is Kilimanjaro's greatest gift to me— learning to live in the single step.

We crest the next hill and then head down a steep incline to a valley. The trail then climbs back up steeply to where Karanga Camp waits for us. There are small, knotty trees with hard wood polished to a shiny luster, thanks to the countless hands that have grabbed them for support over the years. The stony cliffs and rock formations have an orange rust-colored hue, as if they've been spray-painted by God. The hill behind us lacked color and con-trast, but this valley has both. Orange, red, yellow, and black paint the rocks. It's like New England foliage in autumn, except back home that look is fleeting, lasting only a few weeks. This land-scape has worn these colors for many centuries.

Once out the valley, the landscape turns back to muted earth-tones, broken up by occasional dots of pink-and-white flowers on the terrain.

Specks of color dotted around an otherwise hostile landscape—flowers that prove beauty can flourish anywhere.

I use my hiking poles to steady myself as I move around rocks, through sandy scree, and around trees, with their clawlike roots that grip both rocks and dirt and occasionally grab for a foot in an attempt to trip a passerby—at least that's what we tell those around us when we stumble on them.

At the bottom, another stream bleeds off the glaciers high above us. And for a special treat, our personal porters have met us here to take our backpacks up to the top of the hill, where the camp awaits. I haven't seen much of Wilfork before now, but I welcome his friendly smile and offer to carry my backpack up the last hill.

"*Asante,*" I say. He speaks no English, but smiles.

And up the hill we go. The incline is steep, and about two hundred yards long, but we go slow—*pole pole*. As I pull myself up over the last ridge, I see our tents in Karanga Camp. There's one other group, with their tents set up in the lower section.

KARANGA CAMP

Elevation 3995 meters
(13,100 feet)
Vegetation Zone: Alpine Desert
FROM KARANGA CAMP TO:
Barafu Camp: 4 km
Stella Point: 8.3 km
Uhuru Peak: 9 km

The plan is to eat a late lunch, and then Wilfred will take us up the hill about another five hundred feet in elevation to acclimatize, then we'll come down in order to make sleeping easier. Some people in our group aren't feeling well and skip the extra hike. There are complaints of headaches and dizziness, and some opt to lie in their tents. Only five of us make the acclimation hike.

A cloud has moved in over the entire camp and trail above us. Visibility is maybe a hundred feet as we walk. Very soon, I can't see our camp, though I realize it's still close behind us. A light rain flicks at me. A little spray, then nothing. A few drops. My rain shell keeps me warm and protected from the drops and occasional biting wind. I lift the hood over my head.

During the quiet walk, I recall another Swahili word from my college days.

"*Hodi*!" I yell out to Wilfred.

He laughs. "*Karibu*!" he sings back to me.

Hodi is a word that you would yell toward someone's home or camp as you approach. They may yell it back, you may yell it twice after that, until the homeowner or camp owner says *karibu* to you, which means "welcome."

"What is English for *hodi*?" Wilfred asks me.

"I honestly don't know," I tell him. We don't have an equivalent in America. "I guess our closest word would be 'heyyyy!' or 'yo!'."

He laughs. He tells me the story of a neighbor in his village with a vicious dog named Hodi. He says it's a terrible name for an attack dog. I agree. After twenty minutes, he informs us we can turn back whenever we want. We've gained enough elevation for the desired effect. Christine points to a hazy but prominent rock ahead of us on the trail. "How about there?" she says.

It's as good a point as any, so we continue to walk in silence to our arbitrary destination. It's so quiet up here. The slightest shuffling sound comes from our feet. The wind whispers in my ear, rattling the fabric of my rain shell, but otherwise there's total silence. It's the type of silence that calls out to me because in my normal world, it's never this quiet. Soon the silence is all I can hear. There's a music to it. It's quieting my insides.

As we reach Christine's rock, I touch it. Call it a high-five with Kili. A mental gesture more than anything, but it's also an acknowledgment of the hike and the role that the rock played in it. It's strange, but I even feel gratitude for this rock because it's now part of my journey. This seemingly insignificant rock made it into this book. I saw billions of rocks on my trip, but here we are talking about this one, which otherwise would have been like all the others. I note the afternoon's lesson.

The walk back down to Karanga Camp is quick. It's mid-afternoon when we get back to the tents. The clouds that covered us before are moving on. The sun has warmed us up to maybe the mid-fifties. The summit is there. Right there! Nine kilometers away, to be exact. It looks like I can almost touch it. Clouds are buzzing past the peak. I can't help but grab my camera and my GoPro for video. I wander to a higher point of the camp, away from everyone else, and hunker down to start capturing this view and this moment.

I set my GoPro on the ground and let it record. I imagine being able to speed up this video later to show the dramatic effects of how the clouds caress the summit as they blow by and then dissipate. I click still pictures as well. Christine comes over to visit while I'm babysitting my cameras.

She seems down.

"Are you okay?" I ask her.

"Yeah, I just . . ." she replies. Then she looks at the ground.

Out of everyone here, I'm closest with Christine. She's lost both of her parents, and this trip is fulfilling her childhood dream of going to Africa. The reason she's able to make this trip is that her father died a year ago and had some money to leave to her and her sister. I can't imagine the emotions she's going through on this mountain. So we say nothing. We don't have to. The silence is okay.

Sifting through my bag, I find the family photo I brought with me, and the photos of Chris, and the group picture from my daughter's classroom. I also see the list of LLS donor names that I printed before I left. I look over the paper again. Hundreds of people. I look at the names to remind myself that I'm doing this for them as well. More motivation to make it to the top. I don't want to let them down.

Christine and I sit and watch the mountain. Events are unfolding exactly the way they're supposed to out here. Our pace of travel, moments we see coming, and the ones we don't. It's so much to take in, and so much is out of our hands. After fifteen minutes of filming and clicking pictures, I notice a large group of porters and guides congregating by the Karanga Camp sign. They're playing music from a portable speaker. It looks like we are about to have a Kilimanjaro dance party.

I dash down to Tent 3 to stash my cameras and then head up to join the others. Over fifty of us have gathered, with the summit of Kibo right behind us, and reggae music flows from a speaker no bigger than a boot. And we dance. Everyone smiles. It's impossible not to. Although I'm not dancing as vigorously as I might at a sea-level rave, I can sway and breathe.

The recorded music stops, and our guide Sunday leads the singing again, "*Zina! Zina!*"

We all respond, "*Zina!*"

The songs are now both familiar and catchy. I sing along when I know the words coming up, I mumble when I don't. Call it

"Swinglish." I focus on every face I can, trying to sear them into my permanent memory. Our guides, our porters show joy in the dancing and singing, but at 13,000 feet, you can jump around for only so long. As our music party winds down, we drift back to our tents to hang out until we reassemble at dinner.

The quiet is so powerful up here. There are no birds singing, no bugs chirping, no cars or traffic, no jets passing overhead—just a vast expanse of quiet broken only by a gust of wind or the occasional human voice. No one shouts, either. There's an understood reverence among all of us. It's a quiet and peace that I'm not sure I could find at sea level.

That night at dinner, after our vitals are checked, I ask around the room how different people are feeling. "How are you doing, Jason?" I ask.

"When I was lying in my tent before, it was spinning," he said. "And I have a headache."

"That can't be good," I said.

He describes the feeling: as if the bed is spinning, like when you lie down when you're almost-passed-out drunk. Although I've been lightheaded a couple of times, I haven't been *that* bad. I'm thankful that my tent has never rotated in any direction.

"Tomorrow," Augustine says, "We are going to get up at six and hike four to five hours to Barafu base camp. We eat lunch, relax a little bit in the afternoon, eat early dinner, then sleep until eleven p.m., before we wake up and get ready to climb for summit."

Holy shit!? The summit!? Tomorrow! It hadn't occurred to me until right now that tomorrow night we're heading for the summit. I'm not the only one in our group to have this revelation either.

"That's tomorrow?" a voice whispers. "Oh my God," says another.

There's no reason for any of us to be shocked. We are sticking exactly to the schedule that was shown to us months ago. Yet I've been so in the moment, I hadn't considered that tomorrow is the day.

6 SATURDAY

KARANGA CAMP TO BARAFU CAMP

LAST NIGHT, I HAD A STRANGE DREAM. I dreamed that I woke from my tent, turned around, and saw the giant peaks of the Himalayas towering above me where Kilimanjaro had been yesterday. I wrote a whole book on dream interpretations years ago. I've said that the best dream interpreter in the world is always the dreamer, so here goes:

The Himalayas are the tallest mountains in the world. They're out of reach for the vast majority of the world's population. Yet in my dream, they were right behind me. I know I'm not qualified for the technical climb that the Himalayas demand. In my dream, I was at Everest's base camp, so close to the top of the world but not ready or able to get there.

Waking to the reality of Kilimanjaro behind me is a reminder that I *can* handle this one, and also that I need to acknowledge that there are other mountains yet to climb. Maybe that mountain in my dream was a metaphor, or maybe it was a real one, time will tell, but Kilimanjaro isn't going to be the last mountain I face . . . *I hope.*

This relative walk in the park is about to end. It's just about game time now. I've trained physically and mentally for this. I tell myself I'm ready. The Leukemia & Lymphoma Society had matched me with Christine, Brian, Maria, and Gayle, along with our local hiking coach, Sherpa Tom. Tom brought us many miles together throughout the hills and mountains of New England. He stressed the importance of our fitness, our gear, and helping each other when needed. We shared our food, we pulled each other up over rocks when we had to, and we bonded over this big endeavor.

This training kept me focused like nothing before. I'd be out with friends at a pub and ask myself if that double-bacon cheeseburger would help me get up Kilimanjaro. I'd be on my treadmill aiming for a five-mile run. After three miles, I'd get tired and want to stop. A year or two earlier, I would have stopped. But not in the last eight months. I never cut it short. I wanted the summit like a starving man wants a meal. I made sacrifices to get to this point—both money and time. And tonight I will face the summit.

I take a deep breath and emerge from Tent 3. The view of Kibo is the most breathtaking I've seen yet. There are no clouds, and the sun is making it glow golden as its early light shines directly on the summit. This is my first view of the top from the east, so I need to capture this golden glow right now! I dive into my tent and fish out my camera. I'm clicking every angle I can.

I use the camera the way I use my mind. I'm not a carefree person who skims through life; I overthink, I try to understand the world from every angle. I'm not saying that's a good thing,

Packing up at Karanga Camp for our short hike to Barafu base camp—the last stop before the summit.

but it's who I am. I'm owning it right now. Making peace with it, and trying to reconcile this old part of myself with the more enlightened view that I should also enjoy what's before me without trying to think beyond it.

As I stand here, drinking in the majesty of Kilimanjaro, a demon rears its head. In a little over an hour, we head for Barafu base camp, stop for a rest, and start for the summit tonight. This is about to get a lot more difficult. What if I don't make it? I told my biggest donors that I would pose for a picture at the summit holding a sign with their names on it. I carry a printout of those names up the mountain. Now doubt forces me to make a backup plan.

I walk back to my tent and pull the thank-you signs out of my backpack. I ask Brian if he would follow me back up the hill a little way and take the pictures for me. He follows, and I quickly pose with each of the ten signs I brought, plus some photographs I want to hold up for the camera, including one of my brother-in-law, Chris, and my daughter's class at school. Although I don't want to give failure any energy, the doubt has me rattled. I owe my donors something. If this is as close as I get, I want them to see that I tried.

After Brian takes the pictures, we see the entire camp gathering for a group photo. The weather is clear, and this is a perfect time to get a shot with Kibo in the background. The entire army of our guides, porters, and crew crowd together for a group picture. I didn't know it at the time, but this would be the last time all of us would be together.

Brian and I head back to Tent 3 to pack up our things. When I come back out, there's some commotion near the mess tent. Augustine has a stethoscope around his neck. Wilfred carries a chair and sets it away from the group so we can't hear what's being said. Maria from our Massachusetts group sits in the chair. She's nodding, and both Augustine and Wilfred have a solemn look on their faces.

Maria wipes a tear away. I don't want to pry, so I go back to my tent to finish packing my things for the day—a process I have gotten better at performing. I'm now quite good at rolling up my air mattress pad so that the air squeezes out along the way, and rolling my sleeping bag and stuffing it back into its carrying bag now takes half the time it did the first and second days.

When I return, I see that Jason is now sitting in the chair, with Augustine and Wilfred tending to him. Jason is nodding too. Augustine and Wilfred again look solemn. I place my dry bag on the tarp and set my backpack up for the day's hike. The others

Our guides, porters, and climbers posing for a final group picture before embarking for Barafu Camp.

head to the mess tent for breakfast while Augustine and Wilfred head over to talk to Gayle from our New England group. Inside the mess tent, Jason and Maria are already sitting down. There's a strange tension in the air, but I have no clue what it is.

"Well, I'm out," Jason says, breaking the silence. He's trying to be both matter-of-fact and somewhat upbeat.

"Me too," Maria says.

"What do you mean 'out'?" I ask.

"They're sending us down. They won't let us go any higher," Jason says.

Jason tells us how he's been feeling dizzy for two days. He's had headaches and hasn't been able to carry his backpack; a guide has had to do it for him. Maria mentions something about her heart rate being off. Their words create a sadness in the mess tent. It could have been any one of us unable to handle the altitude.

Outside, Gayle is arguing with Augustine. I'm guessing that Augustine and Wilfred just delivered the same news to Gayle, and judging by her body language and tone of voice, she is *not* having it. Gayle was throwing up two days ago; she had a stomach bug and felt like a walking corpse, but she took some special medication her doctor gave her ahead of time, and yesterday she was doing much better. This morning she seems okay to me, but she hasn't been eating much, and I'm sure that Augustine and Wilfred are erring on the side of caution.

Gayle speaks loudly on Augustine's satellite phone to someone. She's putting up a fight. All of us have figured out what's going on at this point. They're trying to stop Gayle from continuing, and she's *not* on board with that decision. I try not to stare, but I'm curious how this will play out. I don't believe Gayle was suffering from the altitude. She just had some kind of bug. I also know, having hiked with her on multiple occasions, that she's tough; she never lags behind the group.

She walks back to us, beaming. She raises her arms victoriously. "I'm still going!" she announces.

We hug her and smile back. I know what this trip means to her. I can't speak for her, but I imagine reaching the summit is a giant middle finger she hopes to hold up to the doctors who told her not to make this trip, and of course, her last insult to cancer itself. Yup. She's a badass. We hug our goodbyes to Jason and Maria. I ask them if there's anything I can carry to the top for either one of them. Jason shakes his head, but Maria pauses a moment.

"Yes," she says. She holds out a small stone that she tells me was given to her by her life coach. She asks if I would take it up for her.

"Guaranteed," I told her. I open my pack and place the stone in a small plastic bag near my personal photos.

Wilfred will lead Jason and Maria down to Mweka Gate and connect with the descending trail near Karanga Camp. They'll stay back at the hotel in Moshi and wait for us when we reach the bottom two days from now.

I'm actually relieved that Jason and Maria are heading down. I feel guilty thinking it, but it's true. Up to this point, our pace didn't matter to me. I didn't care if I got to the next camp at three o'clock or later; I had no appointments, no train to catch. But the summit . . . that's different. The reason we need to leave at midnight is to make it to Stella Point by sunrise. If we have to wait for someone who is too slow, we'll miss a big part of the experience, and of course, we have to get back down to another camp for our last night. Time becomes a factor today. Part of me understands that our guides have dealt with this before and would likely assign one of them to hang back so the others could go on, but these selfish feelings are my reality right now. I'm ashamed to have them. I should have reached enlightenment by now, but I haven't. It's an uncomfortable pill for me to swallow.

Now down to ten hikers, we start up the hill again on our way to Barafu base camp—the last camp before the summit. No longer in two groups, we'll be keeping the same pace from here on. For the first time on the mountain, I'm now thinking ahead. We should arrive at Barafu around lunchtime, then rest, eat dinner, try to sleep, and tonight we start for the summit . . . *tonight.*

En route to Barafu Camp, each step taking me higher than I've ever been before. The air is thinner, but the mountain still calls.

The future is still uncertain, though. I try to get back to the next step. However, between my new promise to Maria, the signs I'm carrying for my donors, and all the people I've told, I'm feeling the pressure of the endeavor. Our group walks more silently than we did on previous days. Even Nancy the complainer has grown quiet. The gravity of losing two people is part of it. Higher elevation and less air are too. My thoughts are turning inward. Each step now feels more important than it did on the first day. No longer a babe in the woods staring at the scenery, I'm focusing my mind and body for what's next.

During our slow walk up the hill, past the point where a few of us hiked yesterday afternoon, I still see the summit clearly.

"I'm coming," I whisper.

Maybe I'm telling myself, maybe I'm telling Kilimanjaro, maybe I'm telling God, who dwells up there.

We crest the next hill and head down into a desolate and dusty valley. Although I was okay at 13,100 feet, will I be okay at 19,341? I recall the breathing struggle at Lava Tower's 15,000 feet. Am I more acclimatized now? Only one way to find out. The valley ahead is full of broken rocks. They look like a million smashed dinner plates, thin, jagged, and piled upon each other. I take more pictures. I want to show this to my daughter, Sophie.

Aesthetic beauty weighs on me because I'm the dad of a girl. There's a lot of pressure on girls to be physically appealing. I think about that often because I want to raise a happy, healthy human being. This mountain is beautiful. It's beautiful from a distance, it's beautiful on the slope, and the view looking outward is beautiful as well. Few would dispute the inherent beauty of this place. But as I walk along some of the paths, I notice the broken rocks, the shattered shale, and the trillions of pockmarks and imperfections that make up Mount Kilimanjaro. I take close-up photos of some of these details because I want to show my daughter that this place is beautiful *because* of its billions of scars and imperfections. I could zoom in closer if I wanted to, and see all of

The path to Barafu, littered with billions of shattered stones looking like broken dishes.

the flaws, or I can pull out and see true magnificence. Volcanic activity, natural erosion, and sometimes violent storms have all shaped this place and left scars, and yet the mighty mountain still stands, and she's beautiful.

When I look at the mountain from a distance, it's not perfectly symmetrical, and neither are we. Yet it's *still* beautiful. With real beauty, you're imperfect, you're scarred, you're misshapen, you're weathered, but you still stand tall for all to see. This is a story, an ancient melody, that I will bring home from this great place. When Mark sees me taking close-up pictures of the broken shale, he walks up to me and hands me a shiny, black rock.

"Obsidian," he says. "It's a Kilimanjaro diamond."

I rotate the jet-black, jagged rock in my fingers. Obsidian is formed when lava solidifies quickly, without crystalizing. The result is black glass. Kilimanjaro made this rock from deep within. I'm holding hundreds of thousands of years of Earth's history in my hand.

"Keep it," Mark says.

"*Asante sana*," I tell him, placing the rock in my pack. I already know I'm going to give it to my daughter.

The clouds around us have gone from a light fog to thick haze. The gray turns darker. I can still see across the valley ahead, but just barely. There are jagged cliffs above me to the west. Perhaps we're about to confront our first real rain. I'm already wearing my rain shell because of the piercing wind. When combined with two thin layers underneath, I'm comfortable. I'm getting adept at regulating my temperature. Temperatures are in the mid-forties, but the wind can bring a bitter chill. Likewise, if the sun pokes through the clouds, the temperature instantly feels ten degrees warmer. Cold to warm, warm to cold, in a matter of minutes.

This valley is a vast expanse of tan dirt and a few rocks. I don't need to watch my step right now. I'm an automaton trudging along. I allow myself to think ahead for a few minutes. To daydream. I visualize standing at the top. Seeing the sign. Barafu base camp sits just above 15,300 feet. I was close to that altitude at Lava Tower, so I have concerns about Barafu's elevation. Still, I've been there. I can do this. It's what comes after that suddenly feels unsure.

Doubt has followed me up this mountain like Gollum followed Samwise and Frodo. My steps are uneasy here. I find myself looking over my shoulder, as if there's a creature tracking me. I try to

We walk in silence through the last valley before Barafu Camp. My journey is turning inward.

focus again on where I am and what I'm doing, but it's difficult. I'm slightly rattled. The relative flat of the valley affords me this luxury. I don't have to watch my steps just yet.

Once across the valley, we're greeted by another rock wall to climb. Its terrain is similar to Baranco Wall, but it is nowhere near as tall. This wall is maybe fifty feet. *Pole pole.* Up we go, inching our way along the slopes and crags of the rock face. Once on top, it's a gentle slope up to Barafu. The yellow dome of the mess tent sits in the distance like a beacon.

I'm getting better at judging time and distance. I no longer think about how fast I could run a distance at sea level. I'm on mountain time and pace now. The truth is, I'll get there when I get there. *Pole pole*. I feel the altitude here. It's harder to walk than it was in the valley. That's the thing about thin air—you don't notice it all at once. It's a slow build until breathing becomes a problem. Remembering to breathe deeper is not something I'm used to telling my body to do. The only solution to gaining more oxygen is to slow my speed and use less of it.

The gap between us and the yellow tent closes. Through the hazy clouds, the yellow mess tent is as far as I can see. The summit is well hidden. As we approach Barafu Camp, there are rocks to climb, stone steps to follow. Brian and I set our packs down in Tent 3 and wait for others to sign in at the camp hut. This has been a minor formality at all the other camps, but because Barafu base camp is 15,300 feet high and the sign-in hut is uphill from the camp, it's a twenty-minute walk.

Twenty minutes to walk across a camp? Really?! I sit for a minute to collect myself. Five of us decide that we'd rather get it over with and then relax afterward. Guide Steve leads us farther up the rocks at the same slow pace. It doesn't take us twenty minutes after all, but it was still a slow, arduous walk. My head hurts slightly, and I'm more conscious of my breathing. Those of us who made the walk agree to sign in those who didn't. By the shack, I can see other tents at Barafu. At least two other big groups.

I'm roughly seven hours from the summit of Mount Kilimanjaro. But I can't see it. She's hiding behind cloud cover. She's up there somewhere, five kilometers away. Just over three miles. If it were flat, and at sea level, I could run that distance in just twenty-six

BARAFU CAMP

Elevation: 4,673 meters
(15,300 feet)
Vegetation Zone: Alpine Desert
FROM BARAFU CAMP TO:
Stella Point: 4.3 km
Uhuru Peak: 5 km

minutes . . . and there I go again judging distance based on another place and time. I might as well be on another planet.

A few people are milling around up here from other groups. Most are resting. I take pictures of the dramatic, yet monochromatic cliffs and hillside. I also take a moment to sit on the edge of one of the cliffs and ponder what's to come.

This is it. The last stop. Kilimanjaro has become more than a place to me: it's an idea, a concept, a test. Can I still set lofty goals and reach them? Can I handle this? So far, yes. But now, being this close, the specter of potential failure haunts me through unnaturally deep breaths. Doubt, which has been following me up this mountain, is catching up.

When I arrive back in our section of the camp, I head into the mess tent for lunch. I'm not as hungry as I had been earlier on this

At 15,000 feet, doing anything takes a lot of breath. I sit and ponder what is coming.

trip, but I eat anyway. One bit of advice that I heard more than once from people who have climbed big mountains is to eat even if you're not hungry, and drink water even if you're not thirsty. So I do. My pants are loose on me. I've already tightened my belt.

After lunch, I head back to my tent to lie down. The temperature here swings wildly. When a cloud rolls in, it's chilly. When the clouds part and the sun comes out, it heats up our tent like an oven. During one of the hot moments in the tent, I lie back and close my eyes. I don't think I'm sleeping, but Brian will tell me later that he heard me snoring. So I must have dozed. Everything I'm doing right now is for my body. I'm lying still because I want to have the energy later. I'm eating for fuel. I'm drinking to keep everything flowing inside my body.

I write a few notes in my journal to document the moment. But I find that there isn't much to say beyond my feelings from this morning. As I write, Augustine approaches our tent for gear check. He wants to see what we'll be wearing tonight. Brian shows his multiple socks, long johns, pants, and rain shell pants, plus his top layers. Augustine approves.

Then I'm up. I show Augustine my heavy SmartWool socks. He tells me I need to wear two pairs. I disagree. I've worn these very socks in subzero temperatures in the White Mountains of New Hampshire. My feet don't get cold; that's not my problem area. He says I need two pairs of socks, so I tell him I'll do it, though I know I won't. I'm not a total jerk about it, so I throw an extra pair in my backpack.

I show him my thick thermal compression base layer and my scree pants. He tells me I need a third layer. I tell him I don't have one, but I promise I'll be okay. My legs have never been cold in my life. My legs are like tree trunks and have been since high school. There's nothing I can do for him here. I just don't have extra layers. Augustine grimaces.

I have four layers for my top: my thermal compression base layer, a Techwick layer, fleece, and a winter shell, plus my balaclava, a thermal winter hat, and my winter shell's hood. I also have gaiters for my lower legs, and ski goggles if wind, rain, or snow whips debris at my face. Augustine seems satisfied, but he's concerned about my legs. I'm not, and I'm grateful for my training with Sherpa Tom in the White Mountains of New Hampshire in the winter. I learned in the bitter cold of New England that my lower half doesn't get cold, but my hands do for damn sure.

BACK IN FEBRUARY, as we did a training hike on Mount Tom in New Hampshire, my hand warmer chemical packs ran out of heat in subzero temperatures. I had to take my puffy gloves off to unzip my backpack to fetch more hand warmers. During that thirty-second process, my fingers stopped working from the cold. I was grateful Christine was close by and could get the hand warmers out of my backpack and get them started for me. She also had to zip up my backpack again and help me put it back on.

The lesson I learned that day is that hand warmers take a good ten minutes to warm up. And they last only two to three hours. When they start cooling off, you need to get the next pack going and put it in your pocket so you can make a quick switch when you need to. I asked Sherpa Tom what I should have done if I had been alone when my fingers stopped working from the cold.

"The only thing you could do," he said, "is shove your hands down your pants and wait until you can move your fingers again."

So good . . . some other hikers come along and see me with my hands down my pants. "Hi, nice day for a hike!" I imagine myself saying to the hikers as they slowly back away. Still, it's a lesson I'm grateful I learned and could take with me. No one will accuse me of masturbating on Kili, that's for damn sure.

I WANT TO REACH THE TOP. I want it badly. I've been think- ing about this for a long time. I don't want to fail. Not here, not today. The part I can control is my food, water, and to some degree, my rest. When five p.m. comes around, the shadows out- side have grown longer.

At dinner, I'm not hungry at all, but still I eat something. It's the first time I didn't ask for seconds, and Philbert, our waiter, gives me a skeptical eye. He's used to bringing me extra food. With all of us gathered, Augustine announces the plan for the evening.

"Go back to your tents for sleep," he says. "We wake you at eleven p.m. You should put your gear on right away, then come to mess tent for some food at eleven-thirty. At midnight, we leave for summit."

With that, the tone of this journey has changed again. The altitude has turned this into more of a physical challenge, and now it's go time in just a few hours. By this time tomorrow, I will either have made it, or not. I don't expect to sleep much these next few hours, but I will lie down and rest my body as best I can.

Our camp goes dark and quiet. I close my eyes as I nestle in my sleeping bag, but my mind is racing. Somewhere in the distance, thunder rumbles. Weather. It's so easy to forget when it's not a factor. What if it rolls in? What if we're in the middle of an electrical storm? I can't imagine they'll let us go for the summit. Then what? Tonight, I do something I've done very little of since childhood. I pray. Silently, in my head, but still I do it. It's not a long prayer. But it's something.

"God? I'd really like to meet you."

It's absurd. But true. It's exactly what I'm feeling right now. If I can make that connection, everything falls into place behind it. I reach for my iPod, which is low on battery. But there's enough to listen for a while. I flip to my Africa playlist and start with Toto. The drumbeats begin the song, and I take a deep breath and focus on relaxing the muscles in my face, my chest, my arms, my legs, my feet, and then my hands.

The song takes me back to when I was ten years old, running with my friends through a Pennsylvania summer by the town pool. Not a care. Buying candy from the concession stand, daring each other to dive from the high board. Noticing girls for the first time, but not having a clue what it means. My whole life in front of me.

"I bless the rains down in Africa . . ." I hear a soft tinkle hitting our tent. I'm not sure if it's rain, sleet, or the wind crinkling across the fabric. It's cold, but my sleeping bag is warm.

"Sure as Kilimanjaro rises like Olympus above the Serengeti . . ."

Olympus is the dwelling place of the gods in Greek mythology. (At 9,573 feet, it's also the highest peak in Greece.) The mythological summit is out of reach for us mortals. Just like Kilimanjaro, yet here I am, ready to make the final push, if the Great Being up there will allow me to do so. I'm aware of a higher power at work here. I have no business being at 15,300 feet, where there's half the air at sea level. My maker didn't place me here. I chose to come here. Not out of defiance, but out of some desire to visit this dwelling of God and the hope to find a lost piece of me somewhere between this tent and the summit.

I lie here in the dark, humbled again by this mountain. Thinking about what will happen in a few hours, trying to find sleep if I can. And listening to Toto.

"I bless the rains down in Africa . . ."

7 | SUNDAY
IT'S TIME . . .

I DON'T KNOW IF I SLEPT OR NOT these last five hours. I'm conscious of people walking around outside my tent. I check the clock on my fading iPod: 10:50 p.m. I'm awake now. I'm trying not to disturb Brian, but I soon realize he's also awake. It's cold. Colder than it's been any other night, but my cocoon of a sleeping bag kept it out. Now it's time to let the cold in, wake up, and dress for the last push.

We're leaving at midnight because it will take about seven hours to reach the summit, and then another three to come back down to Barafu Camp, where we'll rest for a short while before heading down to Mweka Camp for our last night on the mountain. We're going to be on the move for the next eighteen hours.

Last night, I set my clothes near my feet, so now I reach down and pull some layers into my sleeping bag. The more of my clothes I can get on while still in the bag, the less exposure I have to this icy cold. I slide off my sleeping socks and pull on my heaviest pair of SmartWool socks. I slide off the track pants I've been sleeping in and pull on my compression base layer—which looks like yoga pants for a dude (thankfully, I'll be covering them in a minute). Icy, raw temperatures have crept into our tent. I'm shivering as I dress.

Brian switches on the rechargeable lantern hanging above us. It's bright. The world outside is still dark. I continue going through the motions of dressing. I'm following the steps I laid out the night before. One layer, the next, my scree pants, and then making sure that my glove liners and heavy mittens are nearby. Someone knocks on our tent. "Time to wake up," Philbert's voice whispers from outside.

"We're up," I answer.

After unzipping the door, I step outside and feel for my boots in the dark. These boots have carried me into the White Mountains of New Hampshire, all over the Blue Hills near Boston, and all the way to this point. I'm asking my boots for a little more. "Please get me to the top," I say to them. But I'm also saying it to myself and to God. One boot, then the other. They feel cold, but like your car when you first get in on a winter morning, they'll soon warm up and shield me from the elements. The boots are solid and ready. I get the sense that they also understand this is their moment. Feet, don't fail me now.

Outside the tent, it's a new kind of cold. It's about ten degrees. It's been chilly in the mornings, but this is arctic winter. As I emerge from the tent, born again from the hunched fabric vestibule, I'm struck by the view far below in the valley. The lights from the city of Moshi twinkle in the distance. This is what cities look like from an airplane at night—reduced to tiny lights—but

The lights of Moshi at midnight.

Moshi looks different from most other nighttime cities I've seen from the sky. American cities are neat lines of lights in straight lines, or planned arcs. Moshi looks like Christmas lights on a tree. A splash of lights, with very few discernible streets.

My breath forms a fog in front of me as I reach back into the tent for my winter shell. I've learned through training not to layer up too much. I don't want to be warm right now; slightly cold is the way to start, because once we're moving, I'll warm up. Sweating at this altitude would be a problem because I'd lose too much water.

Inside the mess tent, our group assembles. There's a nervous anticipation in the air that swirls with the thin air of Barafu Camp. We eat some cereal, and then Philbert and Victor give us candy bars, a package of cookies, and a juice box to take with us, because if things go according to plan, we won't be back here for our next chance to eat for eleven or twelve hours.

As I eat the hot porridge, my left leg is nervously shaking, like a drummer counting out a beat so fast, no band could ever follow it. This is it . . . or rather, in a few minutes this will be it. I've never hiked this high up; I've never hiked in the dark before. Two firsts are set to happen in a few minutes.

Although I still don't have an appetite, I eat what's given to me, and then grab the candy bars, cookies, and juice to place in my backpack. Outside, I add my winter shell and my glove liners. My hands are already cold, so I open a package of hand warmers. I place them in my pockets so when I need them, they're ready. Philbert fills my CamelBak pouch and water bottle with warm water. I slide the CamelBak in place within my backpack and strap it on, close the clasp around my waist and chest, and slide a wool sock over my water bottle, which is clipped to my side along with an extra hand warmer to keep the bottle from freezing.

Headlamps are flicking to life around me. I turn mine on. I'm typically not a fan of headlamps in the dark because if someone with a headlamp looks at you while they're talking, they'll blind you. I fix mine around my neck and aim it toward my feet. That's where I need to see. I extend my hiking poles to suit my height—I haven't used the poles much on this trip, but now I'll need the extra support. I wear my balaclava and my thermal hat over that. I remind myself that once I take a drink from the CamelBak tube at my shoulder, I need to clear the line of water by blowing back through the tube until I hear bubbles in my pack. If I don't, the line will freeze in minutes at these temperatures.

Sunday, 12:10 a.m. I want to go. Everyone else seems ready as well. Our guides are gathering, and Augustine takes his position in front. "May God offer his blessing over us as we head for summit. Please watch over us," he says.

Amen. It's the first time Augustine's words turn spiritual on this trip—another reminder that this is a different game now. I'll need my physicality, sure, but that alone won't be enough.

We walk, climbing over the same craggy rocks of Barafu Camp, past the shack where I signed in earlier today, past the other tents. We need to cross the entire camp to get on the trail. Far ahead, lights move on the mountainside, a tiny, glowing caterpillar of illumination making its way up the steep incline. Another group. Ahead of them is another wiggly line of lights. We appear to be the last group heading for the summit tonight. With the last tents of camp behind me, it's just us and the mountain now.

In the distance, flashes of lightning catch my attention—an electrical storm to the southwest. Giant clouds temporarily glow from within as lightning illuminates their dark mass. It's tough to judge in which direction the storm is heading, but it's clear that those clouds are at least as high as we are, and if they get closer, this could be a very big problem.

I can see only the pure blackness of the mountain in front of me, and stars above. I can't tell where the summit is, but it's up there somewhere. One step, then another. *Pole pole.* There's a glow around my feet—about three feet or so in diameter. The ground is a grayish-tan in the LED light of the headlamp. With no way of knowing where the trail is ahead, I have to trust that Augustine knows the way. The rest of our guides are either next to us or behind us. One of them carries supplemental oxygen. Yet another reminder that I don't belong up here.

Step. Step. Step. There's no downhill anymore. Christine is directly in front of me. I follow her feet. I assume she's following the feet in front of her. I'm breathing okay, I'm moving okay, I don't feel any aches or pains beyond my lungs begging for more air than they're receiving right now. I want to capture this procession in some way, so I reach for my camera and set it for low light. I jump out of line and speed-walk about fifteen feet to my right to get a shot of the group. One of the guides seems alarmed until he

Unable to see much beyond the few feet of light projected by our headlamps, we walk uphill on patches of dirt, surrounded by a sea of black.

sees the camera. I pull off one mitten, squat, and snap a photo. Then one more. I stand back up, stow my camera away, put my mitten back on, and speed-walk back in line, immediately regretting what I just did.

I've jumped out to take a photo a bunch of times on this trip, but this time I experience a new kind of breathlessness as I try to catch up to the group. There's some slight panic, as if I'm underwater, running out of air and still a long way from the surface. I'm breathing deep and long to catch my breath, but it's not happening as fast as it should. I'm lightheaded. A dull ache forms in the center of my head, and now my chest. I keep walking. I have a deficit of oxygen, as if I just ran a sprint and need to rest a minute, but someone is forcing me to sprint again. I can't say when or even if I catch my breath, because each step takes me into thinner air.

"We're gaining 4,000 feet in just a few hours," Brian says as he also pants for breath. "That's the most altitude we've gained on this trip in the shortest amount of time."

I hadn't thought of that. Everything is exponentially harder up here. The difference between exerting myself at 5,000 feet compared to 6,000 isn't noticeable. The difference between 15,000 and 16,000 is huge. Maybe I can't see the oxygen molecules in the air, but I picture them weighing more than this thin air can hold—like a helium balloon that's losing its gas and slowly and eerily sinking toward the floor. The O_2 sinks to my feet, and farther down, toward Moshi, where it's needed most. I'm trying to steal whatever breath I can.

Augustine stops the group so we can get some water and "pick a flower" if we need to. Unlike our other breaks, there's urgency in this one. He doesn't want to stop for long because if you don't keep moving, the night cold seeps inside. Some people are shivering. It's bitter. Subzero now. It's settling into my bones. It's 1:30 a.m. We're fortunate the wind is minimal.

We keep moving. My nose and face are getting cold. I pull my balaclava up over my mouth and nose. In just a few breaths, my face is warm again. But I have another problem—it's too difficult to breathe through the fabric. I'm not taking in enough air. Every few minutes, I pull the cover down to get more air, and then I pull it back up to warm my frigid face. Still, I keep climbing.

The coldest weather I've ever faced was at the summit of Mount Snow in Vermont when I was a teenager. I was skiing with my dad. We were told that the wind chill at the top was 60 below zero. Until right now, that had always been my benchmark for how cold I can feel. But there was a lodge at the summit of Mount Snow. We could escape the cold for hot chocolate. There's no way out of it here on Kili.

"Happy happy?" Augustine asks the group.

"*Cheza cheza*," I answer breathlessly in Swahili.

We press on. Darkness. Just a soft glow at my feet. It's dusty gray in parts. Other times, there's more rock. I breathe. Deep in. Deep out. Each step takes me higher, to levels of the troposphere where I don't belong. I don't feel welcome here. But not unwelcome either. Just insignificant, like a single ant at a picnic—not worth a worry to the greater beings above.

At lower elevations, Kilimanjaro offered incredible views, exotic landscapes, and enough air to appreciate the beauty of all of it. Right now, she's offering me nothing but a brutal test that grows more taxing by the step. A wind pushes by us and through me. I'm chilled again. Although I ignore it at first, I soon find myself thinking about the additional fleece layer in my backpack. I'm using my hiking poles now because I need all the leverage I can get. Also, I can lean forward on them and rest when I have a moment.

The electrical storm has moved off into the distance and faded into the blackness of the night. It's no longer a concern. I look up at the beautiful stars for some kind of divine inspiration, but they merely twinkle. I can't appreciate them as I did at Shira 1 Camp. I'm too tired. I see the Southern Cross constellation again. I look to it as an old acquaintance I haven't seen since Australia, a friend who might pat me on the back and say, "Hello, mate!" But right now, the Southern Cross and all the other stars are watching me with mild amusement as I try to push into their realm. We both know I can go only so far.

My hand warmers are fading. The chemical packages promise up to five hours of heat, though I know from experience that five never happens. Three is about the limit, and three is about where we are. It's just after three o'clock, the coldest, darkest part of the night. The true witching hour. The temperature is still falling. My core is getting colder, and I need to add my fleece. Augustine calls for another break with even more urgency than our last stop.

"If we don't keep moving, you will freeze," he shouts.

I'm not thirsty at all, but I know I should drink. I try the Camel-Bak, but the line is frozen. Although I was careful to always blow back through the tube, it wasn't enough. I open my water bottle and crack the layer of ice at the top to take a long sip of icy water.

The porters pull out a thermos of hot tea and cups. I tell them no thank you. But I do pull my pack off and reach in for my fleece. I take off my winter shell and add my fleece as fast as I can. The chill of the night startles me to high alert. I add my winter shell again and pull the heavy zipper together to try and close the coat. I miss. I try again. Again I miss. I've zipped this jacket countless times in the past, but now . . . I feel stupid. The zipper even has magnets at the bottom so they naturally pull together to help me zip up, but the magnets won't line up. I can't zip up my fucking jacket! I feel intoxicated. Like a stumbling drunk.

I look up, take a deep breath, and try again. Sunday sees me struggling.

"Let me help you," he says.

In one motion, he pulls my zipper together and zips me up.

"*Asante sana*," I offer.

He pats my arm and moves along without saying anything else. I've lost some motor skills. My brain isn't working as it should. If I can't handle a zipper, how can I handle the rest of this climb?

"*Mwanafunzi*," Augustine says to me. "You should drink some tea."

I trust his judgment better than my own right now. "Okay," I exhale.

They pour me half a cup of warm tea, and I drink it in two big gulps. The warmth passes through my center and radiates outward. And I know the caffeine will help. I open two more packages of hand warmers and place them in my pocket. I'll be needing them soon enough. I reach for the candy bar in my pack and find it frozen solid. Still, I'm able to slowly suck and bite through the chocolate and nougat. I'm not hungry, but I should eat something. I choke down the chocolate bar and try to feel the calories, sugar, and tea inside of me taking effect. I know it's all in my foggy head, but still I send the message to my body that some quick energy is coming.

Augustine is urgent in his orders that we suit up and keep moving so we don't freeze. I listen to him. We're at around 17,000 feet at this point, and it feels radically different from 15,000. Breathing is a strain, even when I stand still. Robert from our group is sitting on a rock trying to catch his breath.

"This is no joke," I say to him.

"No it isn't," he replies.

On the move again. Single file. One foot, then the other. I look to my right, which is north, and see lights from a different town far below in Kenya. At this point, my journey turns inward. I'm faltering. I think of stories that I can tell my friends and family back home, "I made it to about 17,500 feet." I think about captain's practice during soccer tryouts in high school. My asthma was an excuse to tap out. It's not me, it's my asthma. I'm out of excuses here, and though my mother is somewhere worried, she's not here to show or tell me what to do.

My travel doctor's words from last January echo in my head, "You need to be prepared to turn back if you have to." How do I really know when I have to turn back? Breathe in. Breathe out. My lungs are heaving; I'm trying to squeeze every bubble of air out of what's around me. Our centipede of people is spreading out as we struggle. I can't worry about them, and they can't worry about me. Each of us is on his or her own. My hands are getting cold. I notice it in my fingertips first.

I want to switch out my hand warmers, but I'm afraid to stop for anything because catching up with the others seems almost insurmountable. One step, two step. I follow Christine's feet in front of me. My head hurts. There's some kind of stoppage in our train of people, so I take the opportunity to switch out my hand warmers. I ask Christine to hold my poles, slide off my left mitten, then unzip my left side pocket to pull out the fresh hand warmer and slide in the used one. Then I pull that mitten back on. I slide off my right mitten and watch it drop to the ground next to me. I'll get it in a second. I unzip my right pocket and swap out for the new hand warmer, and then go to get my mitten.

I squat and grab hold of the mitten, and then I stand up. Blood rushes from my head, and I'm dizzy. I feel like I'm going to pass out and fall over. I can't catch my breath. The group starts walking again. I blow all the air out of my lungs and breathe all the way back in, the way I would in the past taking a hit on an asthma inhaler. Each step is as deep a breath as I can muster. I don't think I can go on. I'm a child again, suffering through an asthma attack during a sleepover, but now I can't call my dad to come pick me up.

I lean my weight on my hiking poles and close my eyes. But there are people behind me, so I can't stop long. I open my eyes and see that Christine is a few steps ahead of me and moving away. I stand up and step forward. My mind goes blank. I'm not thinking about anything or anyone. I'm outside of myself, moving through blackness—almost as if I'm walking beside myself.

I don't know why I'm still walking. I just am. I'm moving legs attached to a body. I follow those ahead of me, and Augustine ahead of them. I'm lost. I'm nowhere. The only cogent thoughts I have are of my wife and daughter. My daughter gave me a note before I left. On one side, it reads: "If you get tired on the mountain, turn this over." The other side reads: "Just keep climbing."

The predawn sky, offering the first glimpse of light during the coldest night of my life.

So I do.

My head is hanging low, but I manage to turn around for a moment and see the faintest purple glow on the horizon. A single brushstroke running along the eastern horizon, with a slight bulging hint of red in the middle. The sun is coming. If I can just see the sun, I can reevaluate my situation.

Our route turns diagonal to the mountain, a less steep path, and I rotate my head and check on the progress of the sun. It's almost imperceptible, but the purple glow is a little brighter. I turn the other way and see the faint outline of Kili's volcanic rim. I walk on. Another step. My journey is completely inward now. There's some kind of dialogue happening inside me, but I'm not privy to the conversation. I assume that I'm arguing with myself about stopping right here. I'm grateful I can't hear the discussion. I'd rather not know.

The purple is turning to hues of orange and red now as the sun gets closer to the horizon. More light spills into the world, revealing a landscape with no sign of life. Nothing lives at this altitude. No grass, no moss, no bugs, no animals. This is not a place for living things.

It is six a.m. About 18,500 feet. My ribs and chest muscles burn from breathing so deeply. Each minute, the world grows brighter. The rim of the volcano is in sight. I follow Christine's feet in front of me one more step. Then another, then another, until I've reached the rim's edge. Stella Point lies just ahead. It's now 6:38, and I can see the sign that tells me I'm at Stella Point, nearly 19,000 feet above sea level.

Stella Point, 18,885 feet, the edge of Kilimanjaro's volcanic rim.

We take a water break. I set my pack down and turn around. The temperature has warmed at least ten degrees. To the east, the sun is above the sea of clouds far below me, and sunlight has turned the horizon and the clouds closest to it a golden color. A similar gold as my brother-in-law Chris's skin in the sunlight back in December.

Some of the clouds appear like horses' heads breaking through from below. Something inside of me is changing. That internal debate—whatever was being said—is now quiet. The world is quiet. I feel Chris. It's like he's standing next to me. I feel a much bigger being over my shoulder. I'll call it God, the universe, or the spirit of Kilimanjaro herself. I've been granted permission to be here. Passing through the night, I've proved myself worthy. Although Uhuru Peak lies a half-mile away, and another five hundred vertical feet up, in this moment I know I've already made it.

I take a few pictures. I'm hardly looking. I just click. I'll find out later that this Great Being and the mountain have another gift to give me. One I can take home. It's the photo I took.

Hope. What I'm seeing is hope. I have made it through the darkest, coldest, most exhausting night of my life, and I have been reborn with the sunrise. I turn around and gaze into the enormous volcanic crater of Kilimanjaro. There are a few patches of snow, but mostly it's a lake of tan dirt. I remind myself that she's just dormant, not extinct. Still, I don't fear an eruption. I've been granted access today.

Steve is walking around the group and looking us over. He pushes his nose close to mine. There's a serious, almost aggressive expression on his face. "You need sugar," he says.

At this moment, my hope is restored. I've been fighting for breath, but right there, right at that moment, I feel a connection to my creator.

"No, I'm o . . ." I don't get the chance to finish. Steve pushes a piece of candy into my mouth with his finger. It's some kind of sugary, minty confection that starts to dissolve with my saliva. I don't get the chance to thank him, either—he's off to the next person.

I nudge Christine. "Look. The sign," I say, pointing to Uhuru Peak, far off in the distance along the rim to our southwest. Christine is doubled over from the emotion. I'm getting choked up too, but I help her back upright.

Our group looks spent. There are no more smiles. Just pilgrims from the Earth below in a foreign world, struggling to find our strength and breath. The sky is cobalt blue above me, the world continues to warm up thanks to the sun, and the tan sand and dirt of Kibo's crater radiate in the early morning sunlight. The water bottle at my hip is still drinkable. I turn the lid open, crack the new layer of ice, and take more long gulps. I'm not thirsty, but I know I need water.

I fight for breath, but I'm not scared anymore. I've grown intimate with the feeling. I smile, thinking that maybe asthma has helped prepare me for Kilimanjaro in a peculiar way. I've been fighting for air my whole life. Although I'm here partially to reconnect with the child within, I understand it's time to let that wheezing kid go. That part of me can stay behind. He represents the weaker side of me. I no longer need him, or his excuses.

"Okay, we must get going!" Augustine shouts.

It's time to take a long walk around the volcanic rim. The route is gentle compared to the overnight climb. I have my hiking poles, but they're not much use. I'm too tired to use them, and I'm too tired to put them away. I hold the handle straps and let the poles drag behind me as I walk, leaving two soft lines in the sand marking the outline of Jeff's Trail.

The world around me is crystal clear, but my head is hazy. The blue sky, the clouds bright white, whiter than any snow I've seen, the glaciers farther down the mountain glowing aqua blue. The colors are so vivid, but I can't appreciate them right now. It's like I'm drunk. My walk has no purpose, no determination—just stumbling steps that I assume are in the right direction because I'm following the others. Still, I click pictures of the glaciers because maybe I'll appreciate them later.

The glaciers of Kilimanjaro are projected to be gone by 2033. I'm blessed to be among the last to see them in person.

I glance to my left. On the south side of the mountain, the aqua-blue undertone of its wall of glacial ice seems to pulsate in the morning sun: it could be the ice, or it could be my vision shifting slightly in and out of focus. Beyond the ice, the sea of clouds. We're on a lonely island surrounded by a sea of white. A century ago, this would have been an island of white surrounded by a sea of color. Our planet is changing so fast.

I keep walking, poles dragging. *Pole pole*. Brian isn't doing well. He's stumbling. Guide Sunday is carrying Brian's backpack and is holding his arm, escorting him toward the summit. Another hiker passes us, walking back.

"You're almost there, guys!" she says. And she's gone. I don't acknowledge her. I do nothing but keep walking. This is another first for me. On every trail I've ever been on, I give eye contact and a head nod at the very least to any other hiker who passes me. A human, especially a fellow pilgrim, deserves acknowledgment. But the opportunity is missed. She's already passed, and now I'm not even sure she was real. Step, step, step.

Augustine calls for another break. It feels like we just took one at Stella Point. I'm not on my own anymore. I'm resigned to this group—a cog in the wheel. I'll follow where we go. I have never considered myself a follower. I'm an against-the-grain type of guy. I also don't ask for help easily. But on this journey, I've allowed myself to be *mwanafunzi*. A student. Learning again. As I should be in all things.

The water break isn't long, and we're back stumbling along like starving prisoners released from brutal indenture. We lack the strength to run, but we'll stumble toward Uhuru. Then there's another hill in front of us. It's gentle by the look of it, but up here, any rise in elevation strains me to my core. I can't breathe any more deeply than I already am. It's not me walking. It's some supernatural force carrying me along a razor's edge of consciousness—I'm now between the worlds of the natural and supernatural. I'm having an out-of-body experience while still in my body.

I recall what Chris told me about feeling like his spirit was getting ready to leave his broken machine behind. My spirit is now rattling around inside me. I feel it. Although my machine is strong, it's teetering on the red line right now. I step higher, until we crest the hill.

There. There in the distance, maybe a football field away, another sign is barely visible. *That* is Uhuru Peak. The top of Africa. We all see it. There's no joy or excitement. No yelling. We just keep up the slow march to Uhuru; to freedom. I've been waiting for this big moment. I've envisioned it, dreamed about it, trained for it. It's about to happen, and yet I feel nothing; it's just a blind stumble toward the sign.

We're closing in. I can almost read the bright yellow letters on the weather-worn wooden planks. A few steps more, and I don't even notice that other people are still with me. Tunnel vision. A well of emotion hits me in my chest, and I'm crying. Ten more feet to go, and I'm laughing, with icy tears coming down my face. Five feet, and I reach out my hand. Two feet, and my mittened hand grips the wood of the summit sign, confirming I have reached the highest point in Africa. More tears roll down.

19,341 feet—the summit of Mount Kilimanjaro—halfway home.

Others in my group come into focus. Christine and I hug. She's also crying. Gayle is sitting on the stones supporting the sign and crying. Augustine hugs me. "Congratulations," he says somberly, recognizing the reverence of the moment.

"*Mwalimu,*" I say, breathless. He locks eyes with me and smiles a paternal smile. I can't say anymore.

AUGUSTINE ASKS US to assemble for a group picture by the sign. There are smiles now. Autopilot smiles. There's a camera, we're supposed to smile. The group breaks up, and Abel asks for cameras. Each person has a moment to stand by the sign for a few solo pictures. Abel clicks them for each of us. I stand near him and also click with my actual camera in case one of my shots turns out better. I'm not thinking or composing the shot; I just click.

When it's my turn, I hand my phone camera to Abel and my good camera to Christine. Both click a bunch of photos, and then I step aside for the next person.

The area is wide open. There's plenty of room. We could keep walking farther along the volcanic rim, but this spot right here happens to be the highest point by just a little bit. I'm confused, but I know that I have tasks to complete. I have signs to hold up to thank my donors. I have Maria's rock and personal photos to take pictures of. My tasks pull me back into my head. Standing alone about twenty feet from the summit sign, I allow myself to look around through my strained breath.

"This was for you, Chris," I whisper, thinking about my brother-in-law. In truth, it was also very much for me.

"Okay, let's start heading down," Augustine shouts over the wind.

Down? Already? We've been here less than ten minutes, and I still have pictures to take. I reach into my bag and pull out Maria's rock and take a picture with the summit sign in the background.

"We have to get moving," Augustine says, directly to me. The others are already making their way back.

"I have some things I still need to do," I tell him. The look on my face tells him this isn't negotiable. I'm not angry, but I'm also not ready to leave.

"Okay, but please try to hurry, Sunday will wait for you."

Sunday hangs back. Brian is standing near him. I pull out all of my thank-you signs for my biggest donors, and Christine clicks the pictures of me holding them. I'm grateful I won't need to use the contingency pictures I took at Karanga Camp. Then I bring out my personal photos: my nephew and Chris; my family photo; my daughter's class photo; and one of just Chris. They have all made it to the top with me. I pose for pictures with each. I want people at home to know they were also here.

Somewhere deep in my foggy head, I recall the words of Mark Inglis. The summit is only the halfway point. It's here I realize I'm halfway home. Home was always the goal. Not the summit. As I stow my signs and camera, Brian's stumbling diverts my attention. He's swaying side to side, like a drunk at closing time.

"You okay, man?" I ask him.

"Yeah," he exhales.

He stumbles to the right a few steps, and then he's side-stepping left. There's an edge to the volcanic rim a few feet away

I hold up a picture of my brother-in-law Chris and my nephew Henri at the summit.

that would send him down into the crater to his death with one misstep. He's stumbling toward it, and without thinking, I stick my left pole up like a sword and hit his left shoulder with it. I push against his body until I can catch up the two steps it takes to reach him and grab him with my other hand and pull him to the right, where there's no danger of falling off a cliff.

"Dude, you could have just gone over!" I tell him.

"Thanks," he whispers, unaware how close he came.

Christine grabs his arm, and I stay to his left in case he goes stumbling that way again. He needs to get to a lower altitude right away. Sunday sees Brian isn't doing well and comes back to help.

When we reach Stella Point, Brian is faltering a little less. A drop of five hundred feet in elevation has made a difference.

As the summit of Uhuru Peak fades behind me, I have a sense that I acquired what I came here for, but I ask myself: was this the defining moment? Passing Stella Point on the way down, I think I have my answer. That sunrise. That glorious event that's happened every day for millions of years. That simple, daily message of hope from God and heaven above, delivered each day around the world, but it took my ascent to close to 19,000 feet to get a closer look at the thing to realize just how significant this simple event is. I vow not to take it for granted again.

I gaze down the mountain in front of me and focus on my next step. Six days ago, when we began this journey, I forgot to notice the first step on the trail. I don't regret it, because as I said earlier, defining the first step in a journey is nearly impossible anyway. But this next step . . . this next step down is one step closer to home and everything that means.

"You don't have to go *pole pole*," Sunday reminds us. "Not on the way down."

As we descend from Stella Point, I get to see the landscape that I missed the night before. It's desolate, but still beautiful. I'm staring at the saddle between Kibo and Mawenzi. It looks other-worldly—like the lunar surface. A short distance below Stella Point, I find another sign, this one painted on a small square slate:

IN LOVING MEMORY

Michael Gordon

1964–2015

Attitude Within Altitude

Another plaque, this one more rudimentary, in memory of another fallen climber.

We're still above 18,000 feet in elevation; the sign is a reminder it's still enough to kill. It's sobering. I'm ready to come down. For the first time since Lemosho Gate, I'm ready to go home. That's where the journey ends. Not at Uhuru Peak. And not here, where Michael Gordon died. At forty-two years of age, my midlife, I can see that all my adventures now begin and end at home.

The terrain in front of me is full of sandy scree that squishes down maybe two or three inches with each step, almost like powdery snow. Sunday is able to run down the mountain. He runs ahead for fifty yards, then stops and waits for us. I give it a try. If I lean far back on my heels, I can also jog down. But my momentum scares me because I know I'm foggy and tired. I don't fully trust my legs, so I stop about twenty yards down and continue at my slower pace.

Sunday is still helping Brian, but every few hundred feet lower means more oxygen, more clarity, and more focus. He's improving rapidly as we descend. Each breath offers more precious oxygen. The O_2 particles are down here waiting for us, staring at us, and asking why we would be dumb enough to go where they aren't.

The logistics of the day are starting to hit me. We need to get back to Barafu Camp, eat something, then pack up our camp and head down another seven kilometers to Mweka Camp for our last night on the mountain. The route down is one-way. It's intended for the descent only, no matter which route you took to go up. Heading back to Barafu, there are many slips on the loose gravel. My winter shell comes off as the sun heats us up, and soon my fleece is unzipped as we reach lower elevations. Stepping down the rocks and gravel is painful on my ankles and knees, but soon we see the camp in the distance.

As Brian, Christine, and I make our way back into our camp, exhausted, our porters, all smiles, are saying "Congratulations!" to us in broken English. Some offer high fives, others fist bumps. It's just past noon. I want to lie down. I haven't slept much in the last thirty hours. I check my phone and see I have one bar of cell service. I text my wife and hope it goes through: "I made it to the top of Kilimanjaro! I'm coming home." I don't know if the message makes it through or not.

We're told to get ready for a meal at one o'clock. I fall into our tent but keep my boots hanging on the outside so I don't have to take them off or bring the dust inside. I'm not sure if I'm sleeping; I'm just at the edge of consciousness, my eyes closed, drifting but still barely hearing the sounds around me.

When Chris died, the hospice worker told my sister that even though he could no longer see in his final hours, he could still hear us. Hearing is the last sense to go before death. It's the last sense I have right now—just a tentative connection to the living world—and I'm hanging by a thread. But damn, this is a good and satisfied kind of tired.

AFTER LUNCH, OUR GROUP IS CRANKY. No one is in the mood to keep hiking, but we don't have a choice. Still, 15,300 feet may have been difficult to breathe at yesterday, but after coming down from the summit, it feels just fine, *thankyouverymuch*. And we're heading down another 6,000 feet. The trek to Mweka Camp is tough on my knees. About an hour in, on an open plain, the clouds start pelting us with sleet. I put the hood up on my rain shell. Fortunately, the sleet doesn't last, and we keep moving down through the desert and into the brush.

Along the path, we pass several strange carts, each about the size of a stretcher, with an oversized bicycle wheel in the middle underneath wire mesh. We're told that this is how they get those who can't walk down the mountain. Two porters can put someone on this stretcher and jog down the hill with this unicycle gurney. It's another reminder how fortunate I am. I'm not injured. I'm still walking under my own power.

Climbing down the rocky trail, we move into the forest once again. Thunder rumbles in the distance. I hope it stays away a little longer. We reach Mweka Camp at close to six o'clock. At this camp, they're able to give us bowls of warm water to wash up. I run soap and water around my scrubby face and hair and feel somewhat refreshed, but still too tired and overwhelmed to process what happened twelve hours earlier.

After eating and settling down in our tent, I breathe deep and full, languishing in all the oxygen I've taken for granted for most of my life. We're just below 10,000 feet in elevation now, back among living creatures—birds, monkeys, bugs, and trees. I've had enough of sleeping on the ground; I envision the hotel bed back in Moshi, and the hot shower waiting for me.

8 MONDAY

HEADING HOME

MY TENT IS BRIGHTER THAN NORMAL this morning. I must have slept in. Sounds of movement outside alert me that others are already awake. I step out of Tent 3 wearing my track pants and a T-shirt. This is the first morning in a week where I wake up to warm weather. Another sign I'm coming back down to Earth. To Africa.

There's a buzzing energy to our camp. Porters are eagerly packing up gear. They smile. There's some last-day-of-school haste. I learn that this is the last expedition of the season for this group of porters and guides because the rainy season starts soon, so there won't be anyone climbing Kilimanjaro for three months. I look up at the summit of Kili, just peaking above the trees of our camp, and see that it's covered in white. Last night, while we were sleeping down here, a blanket of snow fell on her. She's beautiful in her new dress. I stare. A white-capped mountain in a sea of brilliant blue sky.

On my final morning on the mountain, I awake to find a blanket of snow has fallen on the summit during the night.

Thank you, Kilimanjaro, but it's time to go home.

The hike down to the gate is ten kilometers, but it's a smooth, well-groomed trail, similar to the trail on our first day. We're back in the rain forest among tall trees, monkeys, and vines. I'm walking with Mark, who is Chagga, the original people who lived around this mountain millennia ago. I notice some of the trees along the trail have bark that's clearly been cut off in small patches by some kind of human-made tool. Mark explains that locals come up this trail to gather various plants and trees for medical use. He plucks a two-foot-long, palm-like leaf from something he calls a *Ssale plant*. These plants are abundant on the lower part of the mountain. He ties the long leaf in a knot and explains that in the Chagga culture, if you feel that you've wronged someone, you pluck this leaf and knot it. By handing the knotted leaf to the person you've wronged, you're asking forgiveness. If the person accepts the leaf, you are forgiven.

I take the leaf from Mark, though he hasn't wronged me in any way—quite the opposite, in fact. I carry it for a minute while turning it over, before letting it drop along the side of the trail. I leave it behind as my acknowledgment that I can be a stubborn bastard. I forget very little. This leaf is one more lesson from Mount Kilimanjaro. Let it go. Forgive others. Forgive myself. Leave the emotional baggage behind, along with my footprints.

I have eight days of experience now that has taught me that there's no point in carrying anything that isn't necessary. In my backpack, I always had some food, water, pictures of my family, symbols of some of my friends and well-wishers, and items to protect me from the weather. I needed nothing else. The trail before me opens into a wide dirt road. In case of emergency, responders from town can drive vehicles up to this point to pick up injured people. The sounds of civilization are returning. In the distance are the noises of people working with some kind of tools. There are voices breaking through the thick forest. And soon we reach the last sign. The gate. The end.

I've walked forty miles over eight days, through an array of landscapes and climates. I have pushed myself beyond my limits. I have faced the coldest and darkest part of the night and been reborn with the sunrise. No matter how bad or dark my life gets, I know that the sun will rise again. That's hope, delivered daily from millions of miles away.

Our porters and guides meet us for lunch in a plaza a short way down beyond the gate. Maria and Jason are there to join us. They both wear a smile that hides the sadness and disappointment they feel for not being with us at the summit. There's beer, wine, champagne, and food waiting for us. After we eat, the entire group sings again. This time I record the songs. I'll need to hear this in the future, to transport myself back to East Africa, to this mountain where I'm filthy, dusty, unshaved, unshowered, and yet cleansed.

I'm emotional. We all are. The gravity of what we did continues to sink in. It will take months for me to fully soak in this adventure. Later, I talk to a friend about Jon Krakauer's book *Into Thin Air*. That book relates a personal account of the author's 1996 expedition to Mount Everest, when five of his fellow climbers died on the mountain in a freak storm in the hours after he reached the summit.

"I felt like Krakauer's account of reaching the summit of Everest was so blasé, I didn't believe it," my friend says.

While I agree that Krakauer didn't give much ink to the actual summit experience, it rang true to me because on the top of Mount Kilimanjaro, I wasn't processing what was happening at the time. I wasn't there very long. It was *not* the epiphany moment of my journey, nor was it a single moment of enlightenment.

Zen Master Futomaki wrote: "One does not climb to attain enlightenment; rather, one climbs because he is enlightened." I'm not calling myself enlightened by any stretch, but I get that I'm able to move one step closer to that Zen ideal thanks to this entire process.

Down here at the base, in this restaurant eating lunch, having a cold Kilimanjaro beer, two thoughts seep up from the recesses of my mind. First: *I have climbed Mount Kilimanjaro.* No matter what challenges I face in the future, this is now a fact—a gift that I get to keep the rest of my life. Second: *This experience is now over.* There's sadness. This event, which I've worked and sacrificed for, trained for, and envisioned for so long, is now concluded.

Many of these people, who have felt like family these last several days, I will never see again. Yesterday, Augustine asked if I would address the porters and guides, once we reach the bottom, on behalf of those of us who climbed. So I wrote a letter to them at Barafu base camp. A guide now translates for me. Trying to sum up my gratitude, which I know most of us feel, seems like an impossible task. How do you thank someone for playing such a huge role in changing your life? But I try:

Each of us have traveled a great distance because Kilimanjaro called to us.

Some of us were strangers to each other when we arrived, but all of us were strangers to you.

You have welcomed us, just as the mountain has. We have left our footprints on Kilimanjaro, and have become one with the mountain, just as the mountain has become one with us.

Saying thank you for all you did for us isn't enough. We could not have made this journey without you.

Please know that though we arrive as strangers, we will part as friends.

Each of you has left your footprints on our souls.

Asante sana.

The porters smile and nod. There's silence for a moment, as we all process our feelings in our own way. I get that for some of them, this was just a job, a temporary gig. But they each played a part in something huge.

Augustine makes a small ceremony of handing to each of us who reached the summit Mount Kilimanjaro certificates that feature his or her name, age, the date and time of the summit, and our head guides' names. There were more tears.

JEFF BELANGER

has successfully climbed Mount Kilimanjaro
the highest in Africa to Uhuru Peak 5895m amsl.
DATE: March 26, 2017   TIME: 7:45 AM   AGE: 42

Midlife. Kilimanjaro completed. Not bad.

The dull ache in my heart reminds me that it's time to go home, to be with my family. The end of this adventure is still thousands of miles away in Massachusetts, where my wife and daughter are waiting to hear from me. I'm on my way.

The ride back to our hotel takes less than an hour because we had come down on the Moshi side of the mountain. I'll be spending two more nights here and then flying home Wednesday. All week, I had pictured fighting with Brian for who gets to shower first when we get back to the hotel. But when we roll in, I find I'm in no rush to wash the mountain off of me. Brian showers first, while I let it linger a little while longer.

I'm sitting outside our ground-level hotel room facing a small, tropical courtyard, and the waiter who took care of us last week comes over with a smile. I order two Kilimanjaro beers for Brian and me. I turn on my phone and reconnect to the hotel's Wi-Fi. There's Facebook, Twitter, email, and a connection to my family, all springing to life. It's late afternoon in Moshi, which means it's about nine in the morning back home. I call, and my wife answers. I can hear the smile in her voice. She asks how I'm doing.

"I'm good," I tell her. "Really good, but I don't know how to tell you everything that just happened. There's so much I need to process with you."

I tell her a few little stories, but it feels like I'm showing her a couple of still frames from an epic movie; she lacks the context to understand. The best analogy I can come up with is that on top of Mount Kilimanjaro, I sketched an outline to a painting, but it's going to take some time for the colors and details to fill in. Days, weeks, maybe longer.

The beer tastes so good. Our whole team has vanished to their rooms for much-needed showers. We all plan to meet back outside for dinner at the hotel restaurant. When Brian steps outside post-shower, I hand him the beer. I swallow the last few sips of mine before heading into the room to clean up.

I could tell you that when I step into the hot water of the shower for the first time in eight days that angelic music plays, lights shine down from heaven above, and I am reborn, but that isn't how it happened. That's how I pictured it happening just a couple of days earlier, but in reality, that shower feels like work. Scrubbing everything two or three times. Earlier today, I had experienced body parts itching that have *never* itched before. So I scrub.

I watch brown, dirty water flow off my caked-on skin. As it runs down the drain, it looks like Kilimanjaro's blood. There's a sadness to losing that physical connection with the mountain, but Kilimanjaro's blood has already mixed with mine. We're bound together forever. I left my footprints on her rocky slopes, she left her footprints on my soul—my soul, which feels a little lighter right now.

After I shower and shave, I have a cleanliness that is unique. My outside now feels as clean as my inside. On the mountain, I've wrung out the parts of me that felt dirty. I have been broken down to the most basic part of myself, been judged by the Beings of Kilimanjaro, by God, been deemed worthy, and come out a better man. A man who knows that he can climb mountains.

I'm eager to get back outside, to see if anyone else from our team has emerged yet, and to get another beer. I step out to the covered roof outside our room to find Brian talking to Belinda, his beer almost empty. I wave to our waiter from across the courtyard and hold up three fingers. He waves back, and a short while later, he returns with three more beers.

Soon the skies darken, and a few drops of rain turn into a downpour. Brian and I sit on the chairs outside our room and watch the first downpour of this trip. Nothing like this hit us on the mountain. I can't help but sing a little Toto:

"I bless the rains down in Aaaaafrica . . . gonna take some time to do the things we never had."

There's more beer, more of us emerging clean, hair still wet, but happy. I'm not sure whether any of us knows how we're supposed to feel right now. Augustine and Wilfred join us at the hotel for dinner, where we eat and drink some more as the rains stop and the night settles in, humid and thick. I'm seated near Nancy, the complainer. Even she's played her role in my journey. At times, she's been a pebble in my boot. At times, I wanted to tell her off. But pearls aren't made unless a little pebble gets into the system. I let it go. There's no point in holding on to this minor annoyance.

As the evening wanes, we move to the covered seating area across the courtyard and continue drinking. I have no idea how many beers I've had at this point, but it's a bunch, and yet I don't really feel the effects. Maybe my brain is working so hard to process this experience that my body can't be bothered to process the alcohol too.

THE FLIGHT HOME always feels faster than the flight out. This return trip is no different. Every minute moves me a few miles closer. I miss my family; I miss many parts of my regular life. By the time I land in Boston, I'm cooked the way that one is cooked from traveling for twenty-three hours, not sleeping much, and only eating airline food. But I'm almost home.

Megan rolls up as I step out to the curb with my suitcases, and we embrace. I've missed her touch and her smile. There are a couple of happy tears, and soon we're driving back to our house. Our daughter has an after-school program that will keep her busy until four o'clock, so our plan is to pick her up together, right from the airport.

As Sophie jumps back into my arms and we all climb in the car together, I realize I'm truly home. *Now* my journey is complete. I've reached the summit of Kilimanjaro and returned home—my ultimate goal.

EPILOGUE

This grand show is eternal. It is always sunrise
somewhere; the dew is never all dried at once;
a shower is forever falling; vapor is ever rising.
Eternal sunrise, eternal sunset, eternal dawn
and gloaming, on sea and continents and islands,
each in its turn, as the round earth rolls.

—John Muir

ON FRIDAY, MARCH 31, I wake up to my first full day back
home—exactly eight months since the night I was first asked to
climb Kili, and here I am on the other side.

Through bleary eyes, I glance at my bedroom clock, my bureau,
and my wife lying next to me. I have that vague wonder if this is a
dream or reality, but my jet lag tells me this is all too real. There's
no tent, no Kili, no Africa. That glowing feeling of accomplishment

that carried me the entire plane ride home is gone, or at the very least slipped into hiding. I feel empty. *Now what?*

There's this void. That's new. I've given so much time and energy to Mount Kilimanjaro that's it's partially defined me for the last eight months. Now that it's over, I feel almost hungover.

I lift my foggy self out of bed and go through the motions. The same motions I went through before Africa: fix my daughter's breakfast, make tea, and help get the day started for myself and my family. This routine feels familiar and foreign at the same time. Still, through my cloudy head, I know I *am* different now. I climbed a mountain. A big one. One of the Seven Summits. That sunrise on Stella Point was deeply spiritual. I connected to my creator and now believe that that view might have been like a wink and nod from God. I know, I know . . . I went through all that trouble, and that's all I get? A wink and nod? But maybe that's all I needed.

I stare at the many objects around the house: the microwave, the countertop, my couch, my kitchen chair. All of it human-made. The walls, the floors, and every item inside. It's a far cry from the stunning natural landscapes and vistas that I awoke to just a few days ago. Gazing out my kitchen window, I see the forest backed up against my property. I ask myself why I don't walk back there more often.

My daughter gives me a hug before she's off to the bus stop. As the door closes behind her, my cell phone buzzes, calling my attention to a flood of messages and emails. I can't bring myself to look at them just yet.

We live in a time that's more interconnected than any in human history. But even with that ability to call, text, video conference, email, and chat with almost any person on the planet, I still feel an empty, disconnected place inside that I didn't notice in my youth. I didn't notice it a month ago, either. But I can see it now. Unplugging for my time in Tanzania and connecting only in real life have given me perspective and contrast to the person I was just a score of days ago.

When I unplugged from my phone and Internet and walked among the trees and animals, and then up into higher altitudes, though I was disconnected from technology and thousands of feet above sea level, I felt grounded again. The irony of needing to have my head in the clouds to reconnect with my home planet is not lost on me. My phone continues to buzz. *Not yet.* I'll get back to whomever soon, I promise. I just need a little more time.

I spend the morning loading camera memory chips into my laptop and copying over the hundreds of photos and video clips that I took while in Africa. I need to make sure that I have them all. I need to see that they're safe. I want to see Tanzania again right now, even if only on the screen.

"How are you doing?" Megan asks me.

I stare back at her. Her question, both simple and kind, is far too big to answer.

"I don't know," I tell her.

She sits next to me and I start pointing at the pictures, showing her what I saw each day. I become self-conscious of the goofy smile on my face as I look at all of the images and the people who made such a profound impact on me.

"There's where Vanessa's She-Wee went horribly wrong," I say to Megan while showing her the image of Vanessa holding up her green underwear.

Megan laughs, but she's more focused on me.

Has he changed? I think she's wondering. I'm wondering the same thing.

I said earlier that the man versus nature theme is ridiculous. My story is man versus himself. In all my years, I've proved to be a formidable opponent to myself. I'm stubborn, an overthinker, and sometimes too driven or goal oriented to smell the roses along the way. Sometimes mountains wind up in my path, and other times I place mountains directly in my way on purpose. I placed Mount Kilimanjaro squarely in my path and forced myself to deal with it.

By climbing *this* mountain—Kilimanjaro—I gained new perspective on my place in the world, in the same way that each point of higher elevation offered me a new African view. I learned that no matter how much I prepare and train, there are times when I will end up on my *tako*. I just need to get back up.

I saw the valleys and farmlands of East Africa and carried what I needed: water, some food, and layers of gear and clothing to help me take the next step and reach that day's destination. But I was also carrying extra baggage from childhood: emotional issues and memories that I no longer need and that don't serve me. I saw mountain peaks and immovable glaciers, similar to issues in my own life, things that I figured I could never change. While it may be true that I can't move mountains or glaciers, I sure as hell know that I can walk over or around them. In facing down this midway point of my life, I have accomplished a lot; there's much to be proud of, but still plenty more to do. Kilimanjaro will *not* be the last mountain I climb. *Hakuna matata.*

ASANTE SANA

ASANTE SANA to my family for supporting me through my training and travels, and through the process of writing this book. It takes far less time to climb a mountain than it does to write about the experience. I deeply appreciate the patience and cheerleading of my wife, Megan, and my daughter, Sophie. Megan, thank you for always being my first reader and for your help with the camp sign sketches and hand-drawn map. Sophie, thank you for the notes you gave me to read on my journey. They helped more than you will ever know. I hope you climb every mountain you place before yourself.

To my nephew, Henri, I can never replace your dad, but I can stand behind you as you climb your own mountains.

Thank you to my agent, Eric Myers, for believing in this project and not giving up on it. Thank you to my editor, Kevin Stevens, for making this book better. This project could not have happened without Kevin and the team from Charlesbridge Publishing/ Imagine.

I appreciate my friends and beta readers who gave me feedback on various drafts of this book, especially Amy Bartelloni, Jane Gardner, and Chris Balzano.

Thank you to Frank Grace for all of his help with my photos, and thank you to Josh Gates for being an inspiration and a donor to the cause, and for supporting this book.

We had an incredible support team to get us up the mountain. It started with Donovan Pacholl and his crew from Embark Travel, and followed to the Herculean group in Tanzania, including Freddie Chikima, Augustine Nderingo, Wilfred Ngowi, and many other guides and porters who not only took us safely to the top but who felt like family during my time in Tanzania. This book is my humble attempt to sing the praise of your mighty mountain.

To all the folks from the Leukemia & Lymphoma Society (LLS) who not only made this trip happen, but who made the cause noble, including Laura West, Elise McConeghy, Daniela Erickson, and Amy Hoey.

I will never forget the training and kindness shown to our New England team by our coach, Tom "Sherpa Tom" Calderiso, nor will I forget the friendship and bonds formed with my teammates:

Christine Whitmore, Brian Wyka, Gayle Garlick, and Maria Ciccaglione. We were all strangers to each other when this began, and now I consider you lifelong friends. And to my friend Dustin Pari—though you couldn't cross the finish line with us, thanks for being there for the training. You were with us in spirit.

Asante sana to the following LLS donors who supported my Kilimanjaro climb. I carried your names with me every step of the way: Eric Altman, Robert Bailey, Lauren Bashford, Paula Batzer, Kirsten and Rob Bazuro, Nancy and Ed Belanger, Susan Belanger, Hugh M. Black, Kate Blinten, Russell Boisvert, Chad Brand, Jennie Breton, Christine Brown, Zoli Browne, Nathan Buynicki, Nina Capobianco, Kimberly Cenci, Robert Chamberland, Bill Chappell, Francesca Chiorando, Marjorie Coldwell, Sara Coldwell, Sue Collette, Angie Colwell, Julie Cook, the Corbett Family, Renée Corine, Tonya Cronin, Robert Damish, Bob Davenport, Nicholas DeRosa, Phil Diakun, Staci Dooley, Edward Dorry, Kurtis Dube, Anthony Dunne, Heather Durso, Erik Fischer, Christopher Frascino, GE Foundation, Elaine M. Gardner, Jane Gardner, Josh Gates, Nicole Giacomuzzi, Cindy Gillan, Julie Glenn, Heidi Goodhart, Frank C. Grace, Frank Grace III, Susan Grill, Amanda Grimes, Dene and Jay Hammer, Hugh Hansen, Cecelia Helwig, Leonard Hunt, Joli Ingram, John Judd, Trisha Kelly, Sarah Kitchen, Danielle Lavoie, Greg Lawson, Michael Leddy, Sherry Ledenbach, James Lefcakis, Anne Leong, Sharon Leong, Melanie Levesque, Tara Lorentzen, Kathleen Ludwig, Carla R. Lyman, Cory Lyons, Lindsey Manley, Margaritas Management Group, Inc., Alicia Mastrangelo, Chip Maurer, Drew McGuire, Eric Metzler, Michigan Paracon, Wayne Miracle, Greg Mitchell, Robert Murch, Dr. Luther C. Natter, Linette and Sean Neas, Chiara Ogan, Kathleen Olson, Richard Pahlau, Gena Kay Pavey, Betty and Robert Peckman, Cynthia Perkins, Amanda Perry-Dollar, Rosemarie Petti, Jay Pillarella, Sylvia Pinkham, Heather Quinn, Evelyn Rake, Brent Richardson, Matthew Riley,

Bernadette Rivard, Ana Rocha, Dancing Tim Sands, Aleen Savage, Anne Savoie, David Schrader, Sarah Schwab, Erika Slocum, Kevin Stephenson, Julie Streeter, Jennifer Sucher, Dawn Sutherland, Douglas Swix, Tricia Targ, Debby Tendler, Kristen Tower, Carly Vernon, Cyndi Vojvoda, Alison Vreeland, Jodie Waddington, Kenneth Wade, Margaret Wissiup, Mary Wissiup, Stuart Wood, Jane Woodbury, Christine Zajac, and Amy Zarrella.

Lastly, I'd like to thank my teachers. All of them. From kindergarten through college professors, to people in my life today who don't necessarily wear the formal title. I'm honored to consider you all *mwalimu*.

The Leukemia & Lymphoma Society (LLS) made my Kilimanjaro trip possible, and the Amani Centre for Children enriched the journey. I encourage readers to find out more about these important organizations and support both of them.

Leukemia & Lymphoma Society (LLS)
3 International Drive, Suite 200
Rye Brook, NY 10573
Tel: (888) 557-7177
Website: www.lls.org
Team in Training: www.teamintraining.org

LLS is the world's largest voluntary health agency dedicated to blood cancer. The LLS mission: Cure leukemia, lymphoma, Hodgkin's disease, and myeloma, and improve the quality of life of patients and their families. LLS funds lifesaving blood cancer research around the world and provides free information and support services. LLS is a nonprofit 501(c)(3) organization.

Amani Centre for Children
Moshi, Tanzania
Website: www.amanikids.org

Since 2001, Amani Centre for Children has been a haven of peace and safety for Tanzania's most vulnerable children, who because of poverty and abuse have been left homeless. Amani is a registered nonprofit organization in Tanzania, the United States, Canada, the United Kingdom, Germany, and the Netherlands. Donations are tax-deductible to the extent allowed by law. You will receive a donation receipt from the applicable Amani entity. Friends of Amani USA is a nonprofit 501(c)(3) organization.

ABOUT THE AUTHOR

JEFF BELANGER is one of the most visible and prolific researchers of folklore and legends today. A natural storyteller, he's the award-winning, Emmy-nominated host, writer, and producer of the *New England Legends* series on PBS and Amazon Prime, and author of over a dozen books (published in six languages). He also hosts the *New England Legends* weekly podcast, which has garnered over two million downloads since it was launched.

Always one for chasing adventure, Jeff has explored the ruins of Machu Picchu in Peru, searched the catacombs of Paris, faced down a lifelong fear-of-flying struggle by going skydiving on his birthday, and ghost-hunted all over the world—from a former TB asylum in Kentucky to medieval castles in Europe to an abandoned prison in Australia.

Jeff got his start as a journalist in 1997, where he learned how to connect with people from all walks of life. For his work, he's interviewed thousands of people about their encounters with the profound. A noted public speaker, he's spoken at MENSA's national conference, has given a prestigious TEDx talk in New York City, and provides dozens of live lectures and programs to audiences each year.

Jeff has written for newspapers like the *Boston Globe* and *USA Today*, and has served as writer and researcher on numerous television series, including every episode of *Ghost Adventures* on Travel Channel. He's been a guest on hundreds of television and radio networks and programs worldwide, including History, Travel Channel, Biography Channel, PBS, *CBS Sunday Morning*, NPR, BBC, and Coast to Coast AM.